John Alexander

Dowie

A Helper of Men

THE MAN, THE MINISTRY AND THE MIRACLES

John Alexander Dowie - A Helper of Men
© 2017 Jan Wiseman

This book is not intended to provide medical advice or to take the place of medical advice and treatment from your personal physician. The author does not take any responsibility for any possible consequences from any action taken by any person reading or following the information in this book. If readers are taking prescription medications, they should consult with their physicians and not take themselves off prescribed medicines without the proper supervision of a physician.

A Moment in Time

"For things when they are past are not dead to us but live and act upon
our condition in a thousand ways."

Edward Irving, *The Oracles of God*

"There is a time for everything,
and a season for every activity under the heavens."

Ecclesiastes 3:1

CONTENTS

TIMELINE OF DOWIE

1847	Born in Edinburgh
1860	Immigrates to Australia
1869	Returns to Edinburgh to study
1872	First church in Alma
1876	Marries Jeanie Dowie
1878	Forms independent church
1888	Leaves for America
1893	Opens Zion Tabernacle
1895	A hundred arrest warrants
1896	Christian Catholic Church
1899	Holy War
1900	Announces building of Zion
1903	New York crusade
1904	Leaves for world tour
1905	Suffers stroke
1906	Voted out of Zion
1907	Died in Zion

INTRODUCTION

"Only a small part is played in any great deed by any hero."
J.R.R. Tolkien

DOWIE IS ONE OF the most controversial figures in the history of revival. Some call him "the apostle of divine healing" while others dismiss him as a megalomaniac and a victim of his insane pride.

Who is right? Surprisingly, maybe both. We expect our spiritual heroes to have the occasional flaw; we don't expect them to be the complex mixture of flesh and spirit that made up John Alexander Dowie. At times, Dowie's behaviour would make any believer blush with shame. Arrogant, ruthless and appallingly good at spending other people's money.

But his life is also reminiscent of the story of the chickens in the barnyard. "You'll never get me up there in one of them!" said one old hen to another, as they watched a plane fly past overhead. For Dowie to sit on the ground, clucking disapprovingly at those soaring above, would have been the greatest tragedy of all. A life only half-lived. Safe but static.

Nothing could have been further from his experience. His ministry was one of breath-taking activity, a blast from on high that blew away the cobwebs of a church in danger of becoming a mausoleum.

He believed the world needed a new type of church to meet the challenge of the hour. A church that was radical, selfless and above all, entirely dependent on the gifts of the Holy Spirit. Such a church, endued with power, would evangelise the world to prepare the way for the Second Coming of the Lord.

Dowie's 'gospel' made sense to thousands of Christians, stuck in the rut of powerless religion, and they believed the divine healing miracles taking place at his hands were God's stamp on his message. Christians were not mere observers of the coming Kingdom. They were participants, the end-time army!

It was a dynamic and heady experience. But as the years went by, Dowie displayed a darker, more worrying side to his personality. His confidence in God became a warped and twisted presumption. Until finally, a fall from grace, almost as spectacular as his rise to fame.

The man once described as "God with whiskers on" ended his days a broken man who died alone and penniless. Estranged from his family and shunned by the thousands who once hero-worshipped him.

Yet, notwithstanding Dowie's many faults, his place in salvation history is indisputable. The world is a different place and a better place because Dowie was in it. He may have ended his race corrupted by money and pride, but he didn't start it that way. He began as a helper of men.

PROLOGUE

"I cannot remember the time when I was unwilling to help anyone."

John Alexander Dowie

March 1855, Edinburgh

THE THREE YOUNG BOYS lay spread-eagled on the grass in the pale March sunshine, pensively looking out over Edinburgh. Across the city, chimneys belched out trails of smoke, chasing away the last of the harsh Scottish winter.

Willie broke the silence and hit John Alex a kick, "Cummin up the Crags, Johnny?"

Johnny screwed up his face, rubbing his leg. "That wisnae funny. Wan oh these days ahm gonna kick you somewhere that ye wullny get back up fae in a hurry! Anywae, ahm gaun hame. Got things to dae, ken."

"Ye'll get saft in the heid!" Willie snorted derisively. "Huv ye got another wan o' they books fae that man ye ken? Ye need to watch that kin o' thing, Johnny. Aw that religion stuff isnae good fur ye."

"Mibby ah wull. But ye were bowrn saft in the heid, Willie Chisholm. Yer mither drapped ye on the flair, and ye bounced!"

"Dafty Dafty Dafty," the third boy started to chant. "A big moo coo!"

John Alex took advantage of the scrum that followed to make his exit. Striding over the cobblestones for home, he pulled a stick along the railings, as he chanted out his latest song,

> *Then lit oor songs abound and evry tear be drrrry*
> *Wur marchin through Immanyel's ground*
> *Wur marchin through Immanyel's ground*
> *To fairer worlds on high*
> *To fairer wurlds on high!*

Lifting his voice with the chorus, as best he could remember it, he smartly saluted the coalman's horse, as he marched past the bemused beast,

> *Wur Marchin! Wur Marchin!*
> *Wur Marchin Upward to Zion*
> *Wur Marchin! Wur Marchin!*
> *Wur Marchin Upward to ZIIIIOn*
> *The beautiful city of Gawwwd!*

"Got anythin fur me, Johnny?" A little voice temporarily arrested the march, and John Alex turned to see a pasty-faced scrap of a lad, staring out at him from a doorway.

"Ah dinny ken, lit me see whit ah might huv in ma pokit."

He rummaged around a pocket that seemed to go all the way down to his bony knees.

Ta DAH!" A mint humbug came out, with all the flair of a magician producing a rabbit out of a hat. Conspiratorially, John Alex pushed the sweet into the boy's outstretched hand. "There ye go Jimmy – yer favourite. Dinny tell everybody. They'll aw be waantin wan!"

Jimmy beamed and took off up the close. Any treat was his

favourite. His widowed mother brought up four children in a damp house, no better than a hovel. Mister Wight said she was "a pare sowl" and everyone should try to help her.

John Alex did his bit with his grubby but last, mint humbug.

As he walked on, his march turned into a skip and a jump. It was a good day to be alive. John Alex loved these people, and he loved this city, with its smoke-blackened walls, its dark alleys and its towering buildings. Its castle looking down benignly, yet somehow reassuringly aloof. And he loved Mister Wight. He wis a guid man. John Alex wanted to be like him and be guid tae folk. A helper of men. And wummin tae - like Jimmy's maw.

"Mibby wan day Johnny-boy," his father would say. "Mibby wan day."

1 THE BAIRN SINGS

Old 'Edina'

"Come, let us return to the Lord."
Hosea 6:1

JOHN ALEXANDER DOWIE WAS born on 25 May 1847 and spent his formative years in the bustling Leith Street Terrace, at the heart of Edinburgh's old town. [1]

Those early days gave little indication of the heights to which he would rise - the man the world came to know as "Dr Dowie, the divine healer." Yet even as a child, Dowie had an unmistakable grace upon his life.

His father, John Murray Dowie, moved to Edinburgh from Alloa with his brother Alexander, after their father died of typhoid. Alexander went into the boot trade, while John Murray found work and lodgings as apprentice to the widow of an Edinburgh draper, Ann McFarlane.[2]

Although thirteen years his senior, John Murray developed a romance with Ann and they married in April 1847.[3] Six weeks later, John Alexander was born, followed by another son Andrew in 1849.

Shortly after his marriage, God turned John Murray's life around under the ministry of evangelist Henry Wight. From that time on, his heart belonged to the Lord. He became a passionate street evangelist and lay preacher, working alongside Wight and ministering to, "the perishing in the 'wynds' and closes of Edinburgh and in many villages and towns within twenty miles of the city."[4]

UP THE CRAGS

Much as he loved to tell his stories of *old Edina*, Dowie recalled a harsh childhood, punctuated by frequent illness and poverty.[5] But his short 'bandy' legs and weak constitution didn't hold him back from emerging as the natural leader of his little gang. And when not under the watchful eye of their teachers Charles and John Downie at Arthur Street Academy,[6] the rag-tag bunch would set off on adventures and get up to no good, in the time-honoured custom of children around the world.

"Now let's be men," he told his gang of six-year-olds one day, as they made their way up the 'Cat Nick' to the top of the Salisbury Crags, on the outskirts of Edinburgh.[7]

His pals looked on in amazement when he pulled out his father's pipe and tobacco. "Be careful Johnny," they cried in unison.

But Johnny wasn't one for being careful. He took a long deep puff on the pipe and then another and then another. Suddenly the world started to go round and round in front of his dazed eyes. Dowie recalled the experience vividly, with a tour-guide description of the sights his spinning head took in -

> By the time I got my third draw, I began to feel, Oh, my. I looked at Edinburgh Castle across the valley, and whatever had happened to it? The Castle was spinning around, and St Giles Cathedral was running a race with Holyrood Palace, and Arthur's Seat was drunk. I looked at the Pentland Hills, and they were chasing after the other hills around there, I tried to look at Craigmillar Castle, and it had shifted its place to another side of the lake and was running after Duddiston Church and Duddiston Church was running after Craigmillar Castle.
>
> I looked again at Holyrood, and it was bumping up against Edinburgh Castle, and I looked down in the valley, and it came up and hit me on the nose. I lay back and oh, I was so sick. I vomited everything I had eaten. O my stomach! I should have been thankful to anybody if they had put me out of my misery![8]

John Alex pulled himself to his feet and took a few unsteady steps. The ground came up to meet him again, and he crashed down, gazing up at the concerned faces above. When at length his treacherous legs would hold him up, the adventurer made an unsteady path for home, drunkenly staggering along the pavements. Enough adventures for one day!

JOHN ALEX GIVES UP THE PIPE

Ann heard a noise and found him in a heap at the door. She thought he was sick and bundled him off to bed. As John Alex buried himself under the warm blankets, he decided against coming clean. It was his father's fault anyway; he consoled himself. He should be the one in trouble for leaving his pipe lying around in the first place![9]

After the disastrous experiment with Cavendish tobacco, or 'Abaddon' as he preferred to call it from there on in, John Alex decided he was done with the pipe. In 1853 he solemnly took 'the pledge' with the newly-formed Edinburgh branch of the Juvenile Abstainers.[10]

Assisted by a little bribery with his candy, the young reformer proudly launched into his first ministry, winning converts for the temperance movement.[11]

Served Abaddon right! If there was one thing John Alex couldn't abide, it was being made a fool of. He would make sure tobacco rued the day it emptied the contents of his stomach on the Crags!

THE QUEEN IS COMING!

Life in Leith Street Terrace may have been hard, but there was always plenty of drama to lift the mood. The Dowie family lived only a few streets away from Holyrood Palace, the Edinburgh residence of the British Monarch. And from the first time he saw her, Queen Victoria captured Dowie's heart.[12]

It was on one of her many visits to the city and crowds of people turned out to see their Queen. Captivated by the splendour of it all, John Alex followed the procession all the way up

Holyroodhouse Palace

to Holyrood and watched as the Royal party disappeared inside. He looked on wistfully, with his face pressed up against the gates, self-consciously trying to rub off the ground-in dirt from his trousers. What must it be like to live in a Palace, surrounded by so many beautiful things?

Over the next few days, his little gang set up camp outside the gates of Holyrood, hoping for another glimpse of Victoria. After a few vigils, suddenly the door opened, and a petite woman came out, followed by some little boys.

Immediately the big burly guardsman shouted, "Laddie, the Queen is coming!" Everyone jumped to attention, and a clattering of steel rang out, as the huge, fur-topped Scottish soldiers presented arms.

The Queen was coming. Everything stopped when the Queen was coming.

In one of the few, if only, occasions in his life, John Alex found himself lost for words. He clumsily 'doffed his cap' when Victoria walked past, her silk skirts rustling. She demurely bowed in response. The young princes came after her with their father, lifting their caps in polite acknowledgement of John Alex and his friend.

When at last his breath came back, he shouted out loudly, "Hurrah, hurrah for Prince Albert! Hurrah for the Queen!"[13] The Queen turned and smiled, bowed again, then walked on.

Queen Victoria

His moment in the presence of Royalty passed, leaving only a treasured memory of the "true grace and humility" that characterised the greatest.[14] Victoria was the most powerful woman in the world. Yet not so haughty to fail to acknowledge the least of her subjects. Could anyone stand above Victoria? For all her petite frame, she was magnificent!

For John Alex, there would only ever be one other. An even greater King - one who also stooped low for those he loved.

PASS UP THE BAIRN

Dowie proudly recalled at only six-years-old, he'd read his mother's Bible from cover to cover and prayed every day.[15] That was a powerful witness to the home life Ann and John Murray Dowie gave their sons. They were poor, but they did their best. No one could be expected to do more.

The family attended Reverend Wight's independent church in Richmond Place, where John Alex acted as "the invisible assistant" to the elder Mr Paul, in leading the singing.

Mr Paul was getting old and couldn't hit some of the high notes in the songs. He would take little John Alex behind the curtain beside him, where Mr Wight could see him, but he sat hidden from the sight of the congregation.[16]

Henry Wight

When Mr Paul struggled with a tune, John Alex would take over. Afterwards, the people would say, "How splendidly old Paul's voice holds out!"

Wight laughed at Mr Paul and his young assistant's double-act but kept quiet about it.

Dowie treasured fond memories of his kind and tolerant first pastor and reminisced, "It was the richest kind of reward to be cuddled to his breast and have his loving hand put upon me while he said: 'John Alexander, may God bless you.' That 'God bless you' came down with me through life."[17]

Sadly, there would come a time when he trampled underfoot the wonder of those formative years and rejected his biological father, John Murray Dowie. But neither John Murray nor his precocious son was to know that on a summer's evening in 1854 when father and son walked up the High Street together.

John Alex's legs were in overdrive to keep up. He had been

thinking a lot about God. But he didn't feel God near. Something was missing. Now, for the first time, he was going to hear his beloved minister speak in the open air and could scarcely contain his excitement.

When Wight's portable wooden pulpit came into view, his heart beat like a drum. A crowd of people surrounded Wight outside of John Knox's house, just down the street from St Giles Cathedral. John Alex knew the place well. He had been through every close and alleyway in the 'Royal Mile' and heard all the stories from Scotland's turbulent history.

But that night things seemed different. In the twilight, the stars shone resplendent, as he had never seen them before.[18]

From his vantage point, Wight saw father and son approach and shouted down, "Pass the bairn up to me!"[19]

Suddenly everything began to move in slow motion. Something strange was happening. The people didn't make him afraid; he felt surrounded by something bigger than his fear. Yet something powerful stirred deep in his spirit. It was a holy moment. A God moment.

Wight stood John Alex beside him in his little street pulpit and encouraged, "Johnny sing!"

John Alex asked, "What shall I sing?" "Come let us return to the Lord our God," Wight replied. "To the tune of Martyrdom."

John Alexander Dowie's loud, clear voice rang out in the High Street with the words,

Come let us to the Lord our God
With contrite hearts return
Our God is gracious
Nor will leave, the desolate to mourn.

A holy hush descended upon the on-lookers, as his voice echoed from the surrounding high houses, "from the very house where John Knox had lived and from the steps on which he preached. It echoed from the Tron Kirk, a sacred spot where many martyrs had died for the Christ."[20]

As he looked down at the watching crowds, John Alex saw people were weeping all around him. He was crying too, but he didn't know why. Wight wiped away his tears and said, "Now, Johnny, sing to them,"

Long hath the night of sorrow reigned
The dawn shall bring us light
God shall appear, and we shall rise
With gladness in his sight.[21]

The little boy sang on. When he looked up in the night sky, all at once "the Face" he had so longed to see, seemed to look down upon him, with the stars, "like jewels in his robe; the purple and white of the sky as a royal robe around his breast."[22]

It was a moment in time that changed his life, the lives of thousands he would minister to worldwide and millions more touched by the spreading flames of the Pentecostal message.

THE HELPER OF MEN

He ran home and excitedly told his friends of "the Face" he saw in the sky. "The Christ was there, and I rose with gladness," he told them. "I believe that I am converted. I saw the Christ!"[23]

The sense of awe from that moment lingered on, and a few days later he asked his father what his name meant. He had been reading the Bible, and the people there all seemed to have names that meant something. He was sure that his name would mean something too!

John Murray proudly told his son the name was always in their family. The Dowies were Covenanters who fought under the flag of a Little White Dove, in the days of 'Bloody Clavers' who persecuted the Scottish church.[24] 'John Alexander' was in the Bible, but John Murray didn't know what it meant.

With his imagination fired, John Alex poured over his Bible dictionary, until he found what he was looking for - *"John Alexander, by the grace of God, a helper of men."*[25]

A tremor ran through him and finding a quiet little spot, he whispered the words "God if you will help me, I will be a helper of men."

It was the very best thing that he could ever imagine. To be a helper of others was surely the greatest calling of all.[26]

REVEREND WIGHT

We need to leave little John Alex Dowie with his prayers for a moment to consider the people God put around him at that time because they would be important to his later ministry.

Many Pentecostal scholars today would agree with Kenneth

MacKenzie's description of Dowie as "unquestionably the Apostle of Divine Healing in his day."[27] But what are less clear are the links between Dowie and those who went before him, notably Edward Irving.

That is important because, as Vinson Synan commented, "The roots of all modern healing movements lie in Europe where healing in answer to prayer was first taught by Presbyterian Edward Irving in London (1830)."[28]

Synan's observation is well-made. Often the Pentecostal movement presents itself as almost a spontaneous occurrence in salvation history. That is incorrect, both from a theological and a historical standpoint and Henry Wight is a key figure to understand how Irving's teachings may have first influenced Dowie.

Edward Irving

As a young man, Henry Wight was an affluent law graduate, whose life was devastated when he killed his wife in a tragic accident.[29] Through his grief, he came to Christ under Edward Irving's preaching when he was saved in 1827.

Wight embraced his new faith enthusiastically and became an elder in a church in Edinburgh, run by the Reverend Walter Tait, a keen supporter of Irving.[30]

Irving was one of the best-known ministers of his day, but his beliefs were not always popular with the wider church. He taught that the "primitive church" practised all the gifts of the Holy Spirit and it was only through a lack of faith these had fallen away.[31] According to Irving, God was just as willing today to give miraculous powers to his church and indeed would do so in the "Last Days."

That led to a great raft of discussion what those Last Days would be like and a longing to move in the power of the 'primitive church' once more, through the mysterious baptism in the Holy Spirit.

THE PORT GLASGOW PENTECOST

God answered that cry in 1830 when Tait and Wight became part of the group connected with the *Port Glasgow Pentecost* - a dramatic outpouring of the Holy Spirit in the West of Scotland.

The move of God was marked by divine healing, speaking in tongues and vivid prophecies of a promised spiritual outpouring, when Christ would come and inhabit his church.[32]

They thought this was a prophecy of the end-time outpouring of the Spirit which would equip the church for action and prepare the way for the Second Coming of the Lord.[33]

The Port Glasgow Pentecost was one of the most significant moves of God of the nineteenth century. Unfortunately, these early charismatics quickly fell into division when 'apostles' from Irving's London-based church wanted to take control, and the spirited Scottish prophets would have none of it.[34]

The Scottish church excommunicated virtually all of the Presbyterian ministers associated with the outpouring, including

Irving. Wight's pastor Walter Tait joined Irving's new movement, the Catholic Apostolic Church,[35] but the minister linked to the initial move of God, John McLeod Campbell, refused the offer and instead became an independent pastor.

Though very much a part of the charismatic Port Glasgow group, Wight had second thoughts when he saw divisions emerge. For him, they were an "evil in the midst of good."[36] He decided to separate from the others and became an independent evangelist, and later a Congregational minister.

His evangelism met with success, and in 1832 he formed a church for his converts to fellowship in at Richmond Place in Edinburgh. Although the church grew to about four hundred strong,[37] twenty years on Wight's portable wooden pulpit was still a regular feature on the streets of Edinburgh, often pitched in the doorway of a tavern to shame away the customers.

As Wight preached, young men from his church would gather around, singing psalms and witnessing to the crowds, with little John Alex Dowie in the midst of them.[38]

No one was idle in Henry Wight's church. It was "a spiritual hive and every day and night - there went out from it busy workers in all departments of Christian service."[39]

How much detail from his early days as a Christian Wight passed on to his converts is uncertain. But Dowie evidently knew his testimony that "through Edward Irving's wonderful ministry that so thrilled Scotland he was converted and threw all his talents and time, his wealth and social strength, into the ministry of Christ."[40]

There is also evidence Wight's church retained a connection with John McLeod Campbell.[41] Dowie's confidence in the "larger hope" (the idea that there is still an opportunity for restitution after death) was unusual amongst the circles Dowie later moved in, but very much in keeping with beliefs held by McLeod Campbell.[42] Indeed there are traces of Irving and McLeod Campbell's 'Incarnational theology' throughout Dowie's preaching.[43]

Likewise, the similarities between his first pastor and Dowie's early days in ministry are striking. Both Congregational ministers, street preachers and temperance supporters. Equally striking, if not even more so, are the similarities between the message of the Port Glasgow prophets and Dowie's later eschatological beliefs.[44] Namely that God would pour out his Spirit in the Last Days revival to prepare the way for the Second Coming of the Lord.[45]

These are valuable insights into the spiritual world Dowie inhabited as a young boy and indicate that his beliefs in the gifts of the Holy Spirit were not entirely a later development.

Although the establishment of the Scottish church vilified McLeod Campbell and Irving, great thoughts take on a life of their own, worked out through the most unlikely of people!

AN ABSURD AND MONSTROUS LIE!

Which takes us back to our little John Alex Dowie in Leith Street Terrace, Edinburgh. An unremarkable little boy in outward appearance but with a tremendous capacity to learn.

Although chronic dyspepsia led to frequent absences from school, he diligently studied books lent to him from well-meaning friends. And even at this early stage, his knowledge far surpassed other children of his age.

But that didn't mean he agreed with everything he read. Pouring over his books, he decided that ideas about Calvinism were good – but sometimes not that good. How would anybody get saved if these preachers kept telling them they might go to Heaven, or they might not? Who could be sure?

John Alex was sure – he was going to Heaven. One evening, his father's friends huddled around the fire, discussing election and predestination.

His hackles rose when he overheard their conversation. How could they believe that God Almighty from all eternity had predestined some people to be damned and some people to be saved? Whatever they did, good or bad, it was all decided before they were born! It was "an absurd and monstrous lie!"[46]

The adults moved on to deliberating "oblivion" - a new word for John Alex. He sat quietly listening on, but inside was bursting to join the discussion. The Reverend Johnson, Chaplain of Edinburgh Jail, saw his furrowed brow and asked, "What does the laddie think?"

The laddie had "an opinion all ready" -

> As I sat there and listened, I studied the word "oblivion." I had found that oblivion meant utter forgetfulness, utter annihilation. I was sitting thinking about all these things when they asked me

what I thought about it all. I said, "Mr Johnson, I think the best thing to do would be to throw the whole thing into an Ocean of Oblivion."[47]

The men listened with incredulity at John Alex's impassioned speech. John Murray laughed nervously, "Aye, dinny ask him whit ye dinny want tae ken, fur he wull tell ye!" The others smiled and went back to their tea. He was just a little boy, what did he know?

GRACE AND IMPATIENCE

The little boy grew up. As Ann and John Murray looked on, they couldn't help but wonder where they got him from! John Alex was such a strange mixture of grace and impatience. For all his short stature, he seemed to stand head and shoulders above those around him. And such a temper. He would take on the Devil. Everybody knew that – maybe even the Devil himself!

Ann smiled when she remembered just the other day John Alex came running home from school with his clothes all muddied, after scrapping with Willie Chisholm, the class bully.[48] John Alex was sweet on Bessie, but Willie kept picking on the poor girl. Bessie's chivalrous defender decided the time had come to give Willie a kicking that he wouldn't forget in a hurry.

"I could lick you with my left hand," Willie scornfully mocked, as he reached out to yank Bessie's hair again. Within a moment, he found himself flat on his back and begging for mercy, as John Alex laid into him yelling, "Will you give in? Will you never do it again, you coward?"

John Alex kept kicking Willie until he extracted a promise

never to annoy Bessie again. And then he kicked Willie a good few times more, just for good measure!

The other boys listened in amazement when Willie told them the diminutive Dowie defeated him in battle. He lowered his voice to a stage whisper, surreptitiously glancing over at Dowie. "It wasn't only the licking he gave me but the way he looked at me! That Johnny has seven devils in him!"[49]

John Alex laughed all the way home. Devils! He didn't have any devils in him. If anyone had devils, it was Willie. John Alex had God. That's how the little weakling beat Willie Chisholm. And that's how the little weakling would beat any other bully who hurt people he loved.[50] John Alex didn't like people messing with the people he loved. He was a helper of men – and women. Especially Bessie, he told his mother, as she grimaced at the rip in his good trousers.

Now alone with her thoughts, Ann looked around the near empty room. So many memories. Some good, some bad. *The things that are past are not dead to us but live and act upon our condition in a thousand ways.* She thought she remembered someone said something like that. Anyway, it was true.

Ann had many memories of her little home. Some so happy - that night when Johnny came running back to tell her he saw God in the sky! Some too sad to be brought to mind for long. The time when he kept those tragic newspaper stories from journalist William Howard Russell, during the Crimean War.[51]

She shuddered when she remembered the pitiful sight of the famous Black Watch come up the Lawn Market and High Street with only a hundred able-bodied men after three thousand went off to war. She wished she hadn't let John Alex watch that sad homecoming parade. He was such a strange boy. Who knew what went on in his head?

Ann drew her breath in and straightened her shoulders. He was her boy. And he was smart. Her John Alex was going to go far. Just the other day, he won the *Dux* award at school.[52] Her boy the top student, and she could scarcely read![53] He could say as many big words as he liked. He was her boy, and she was proud of him!

Rousing herself from her daydreaming, Ann went back to her packing. It was December 1860, and the family were about to leave Edinburgh to live with another Alexander - her brother-in-law in Australia.[54]

She hoped John Alex would get on with his relatives. "Best to mind your own business and not upset anyone," she always told him.

Not that he ever listened.

2 THE STUDENT

The young Dowie

"All I believe and a great deal mair!"
John Stuart Blackie

ON ARRIVAL IN AUSTRALIA Dowie started work for his Uncle Alexander in the South Australian Boot Factory in Rundle Street, Adelaide.[1] Alexander was an altogether different personality type from his amenable brother John Murray. In truth, much more akin to his nephew and namesake.

As a self-made man in his opinion, a little hard graft never hurt anyone. So Dowie went to work in Alexander's factory for eight shillings a week, cleaning stock, sweeping floors, grooming horses, mucking out stables and hauling leather around the factory.[2]

Two Dowie men, cut from the same cloth, were never going to make for a happy working relationship and it was no big surprise to anyone when sparks began to fly. An argument over a handful of envelopes saw them almost come to blows. They sized each other up, like bulls ready to charge, with their Celtic blood boiling. Neither was willing to give way but the younger, menacingly, held a bootjack in his hand![3]

Alexander thought the better and walked away. A pile of envelopes was no reason to spill blood - still that boy was wild. If he weren't family, Alexander would have sacked him a long time ago. With a temper like that, he was heading for the gallows![4]

DOWIE BRINGS THE LIGHT

After four months in the Boot Factory, Dowie decided it was time to move on. He resigned and started a new job as a clerk with G & R Wills Wholesale Dry Goods, at a pound a week. A canny talent for business led to responsibility for transactions of a yearly two million dollar turnover of business, a junior partnership and then appointment to financial manager.[5]

The young entrepreneur acquired a taste for success and decided he could do more. With the money saved from his increased income, he bought a share in a hardware company, handling government contracts to supply pipes for water and gas.[6]

It was a good move because opportunity came knocking when the gas-works of Adelaide blew out, plunging the whole city into darkness. Always on the lookout for a healthy profit margin, Dowie discreetly bought up all the lamps and kerosene oil on the market so that everyone had to buy them from his company! He didn't see anything wrong in that. After all, it was a public service to keep the city in light, and somebody had to do it. Why not him?[7]

But there was more to life than just making money. During this time, he played an active part in Hindmarsh Square Congregational Church, led by the Reverend Francis William Cox. According to E.S. Kiek, he "loved to attend all of the classes and meetings" and no one could rival his knowledge of Scripture, with a grasp of subjects beyond the attainment of anyone else of his age.[8]

Alongside his church work, Dowie was a keen supporter of the Adelaide temperance movement with his father John Murray, now a Deacon at Hindmarsh Square.[9]

But the sickness that had blighted his life since childhood held him back and often left him debilitated and unable to walk any distance. When somebody told him to pray, he mulled the thought over in his mind. Could God still heal today? All his life, he had taken medicine, with nothing to show for it. He was weak, emaciated and thoroughly fed up being sick. Did God not make his body? Why then could he not heal it?

A breakthrough came when he decided to give it all over to God,

> One night I said, That is not the way to get healing, if my watch went wrong I should not take it to a blacksmith, but I would take it to a watchmaker, my

body has gone wrong and the Lord knoweth my frame. He remembereth that I am dust and I will go to him, and I will never take another drop of medicine while I live.[10]

The next morning he awoke to feel much better and, for the first time in weeks, went for a long walk, hungrily eating fruit picked from their garden. On return, much to her amazement, Dowie devoured an extra-large bowl of his mother's porridge! He later wrote,

> I was healed—a wonderful thing had come to me! I did not know, and I did not talk, much about it. Those were days in which I did some thinking and not much talking![11]

Dowie never went back to his medicine bottles. Little did he know then though, he would tell his story to countless people across the world to encourage them to believe God for their own divine healing.

BACK TO AULD REEKY

Despite flourishing in his adopted country, Dowie was restless. His heart was set on a better education to become a full-time minister. John Murray had high hopes for his son and encouraged him in his dreams of ministry.[12]

But at that time Australia was not well-established in educational institutions, and with no suitable theological college to attend, his thoughts turned back to Scotland. After two years with a private tutor preparing for university, finally Dowie was ready to enrol in the prestigious Edinburgh University.[13]

In 1869, he set sail for Scotland. He had come far and not just geographically. Back in *Auld Reeky*, no longer the little boy with no knees in his 'troosers' - now a young man with a great future ahead of him. As he walked down the familiar streets, armed with his books, just for a moment, Dowie let himself get a little bit sentimental. Looking up at the Salisbury Crags, he thought back to the days up there with his gang.

Where were they now? Would he meet them again? What had become of them? Willie's voice drifted down from the distance. "Aw they books wull make ye saft in the heid Johnny!"

"Mibby they wull," he quietly whispered to nobody in particular. "Mibby they wull. But ah'll still gie folk like you a kickin' Willie Chisholm!"

A GREAT DEAL MAIR!

Dowie was determined to get the very best out of his time back in Scotland and alongside his University studies, enrolled in theological classes at the Free Church College.

His days were full and his mind teeming with new ideas. When out of class, he worked in the Carrubbers Close Mission with James Gall, preaching in the Whitefield Chapel and editing their mission journal. He also held a position as lay chaplain at Edinburgh Infirmary and Thomas Guthrie, social reformer and champion of the *Ragged Schools*, he counted a close and "intimate" friend. Evenings were spent street preaching "near the steps of John Knox's house and under the shadow of the Tron Kirk."[14]

Although steeped in Presbyterian theology, Dowie believed

salvation was a choice to be made, not a predetermined destiny. He quoted with approval Robert Burns' scathing attack on 'the elect' of hyper-Calvinism,

> *Holy Willie said, according to Burns in his poem,*
> *"O Thou, wha in the heavens dost dwell,*
> *Wha, as it pleases best thysel*
> *Sends ane to heaven and ten to hell."* [15]

John Stuart Blackie

Dowie held fast to his early belief that it was a great error to hold that anyone could be damned or saved, regardless of what they did.

He wasn't alone in that view and related the good-humoured dialogue that took place when they told his Greek lecturer John Stuart Blackie he must sign the Westminster Confession of Faith to take up his Chair at the University

And he said, 'How can I sign that?' Everybody knew he was very loose upon some points.

Well, you cannot take your chair until you sign it.'

'Well, now' he said, 'Mr Kennedy, what does it mean to sign it?'

'Well, it means this, that you are to sign that Confession of Faith and say that it contains what you believe.'

34

He replied, 'Twill do that quickly. Give me a pen.'

Then he sat down, and he wrote, 'John Stuart Blackie.' But as he did so he said, 'This contains all that I believe and a great deal mair.'[16]

Dowie echoed Blackie on the Confession of Faith,

> It contains all I believe and a great deal mair, and the only thing about it is the "great deal mair"—especially when it wants me to believe the eternal reprobation of unbaptised infants and in the foreordination to damnation of people without any possibility of Salvation. I will not believe it. I will not believe it, and I told my father that when I was a little fellow.[17]

Both Blackie and Dowie knew the problem with theology was that "a great deal mair" tends to get added to it. And with each new generation of theologians, a fresh infilling of "a great deal mair." Before you knew it, salvation came from the creed, rather than from the Lord! As far as Dowie was concerned, doctrine wasn't bad, but it wasn't perfect either. If it wasn't in *the Book* - it wasn't in his book. He was no Holy Willie hypocrite. He was an evangelist – a helper of men.

IT'S A LIE!

After his first year in Edinburgh, Dowie had his eye on finishing his studies in Germany at the University of Berlin. He put everything in place to go but at the last moment hostilities in Europe through the Prussian War made travel impossible.

The setback led to a revision of plans and enrollment in a

second year at Edinburgh University in Moral Philosophy under Henry Calderwood and Logic classes under Alexander Frasier.[18]

That proved for an interesting mix and brought out the Dowie fighting spirit. Calderwood's best-known work *The Philosophy of the Infinite* (1854) attacked the influential thesis of former Edinburgh University Logic professor Sir William Hamilton there can be no knowledge of the Infinite.

By way of contrast, Alexander Frasier, who studied under Hamilton, now held the Chair in Logic and Metaphysics at the University.

Hamilton had fixed a plaque on the wall in the lecture room with his maxim engraved on it - *On earth, there is nothing great but man, in man there is nothing great but mind.*

Dowie eyed it up suspiciously every time he walked into class. He didn't like it. It was ungodly and untrue! His moment came when Professor Frasier asked the class to give an extemporaneous address on thoughts connected with Logic and Metaphysics.

When it came to his turn, Dowie calmly said, "I desire to criticise the motto above your head, Professor Frasier. It is a lie."

A gasp of shock ran through the room. Dowie went on, "I don't care who said it." "Sir William Hamilton," the other students immediately shouted back.

Undaunted, Dowie continued,

> I don't care whether it was Sir William Hamilton or anybody else. It is a lie to say that in man there is

nothing great but mind because there is a spirit in man and it is far greater than mere mind. The mind of a magnificent man might not only suffer a collapse but be plunged into hopeless darkness, chaos and ruin. A splendid man may become a drivelling idiot by a blow and his mind, his mental powers, not only become empty but degenerate and thrown into confusion but the majestic spirit of that man would remain.[19]

He took his seat again; glad he had said his piece. For Dowie, a person's spirit was so much greater than their physical being. People were created in the image of God. That made it obvious to him that Hamilton's words were totally illogical!

Others might compromise but never Dowie. He had a fire in his bones, a holy boldness. The little boy who told Reverend Johnston what he thought about 'Oblivion' had grown up. But he still had an "opinion all ready" and delivered it boldly, whenever he got the chance.

THE DOCTORS

During these early years, Dowie showed little of the animosity he later displayed to the medical profession. He knew Sir James Simpson personally through Simpson's voluntary work at Carrubbers Mission and held him with the greatest respect.[20]

Simpson was a world-renowned doctor, pioneer of chloroform and physician to Queen Victoria, yet also a born-again Christian who ran a free clinic for the poor at Carrubbers Mission. When asked what his greatest discovery was, he replied, "That I am a great sinner and that Jesus is a great Saviour!"[21]

So it was not medicine itself that infuriated Dowie in these early days, but rather the blind faith people put in doctors when often only a miracle could save them. As chaplain to the surgical and medical wards of Edinburgh Infirmary, he was "acquainted with griefs."[22] He saw first-hand the heartbreak of those who had trusted so much in medicine, only to be left shattered at the loss of a loved one.

At the same time, he sat in on the clinics of the surgeons of the Infirmary and heard them say they were often groping in the dark to cure people. In one lecture, he heard Professor Douglas MacClagan tell medical students if they came to hear him speak on medicine as a science, they would be disappointed. MacClagan went on,

> From the days of Hippocrates and of Galen until now, we have been stumbling in the dark, from diagnosis to diagnosis, from treatment to treatment and we have not found the first stone that we can lay as a foundation for medicine as a science.[23]

Dowie was caught up in the tension between the youthful arrogance of 'modern' medicine and the eternal wisdom of the Creator. For his logical mind, medicine could not possibly be scientific, since theories of medicine changed every few years.[24] And if medicine wasn't a science, then it followed medicine had no claim to assert its exclusive authority over sickness. It was just another absurd and monstrous lie!

DOWIE MAKES HIS STAND

The anger against the secularisation of medicine welled up in his spirit. No one seemed to speak out against it! The church sat back in silence when doctors dismissed the idea that God could heal. Yet, Dowie reasoned, if God created the body, could he not also restore that body from sickness?

One day he sat listening as the distinguished Congregational minister and Professor of Theology at Edinburgh University Dr Lindsay Alexander gave a lecture on 1 Corinthians 12. When he reached the gifts of healings, Alexander said, "These Gifts have passed away."[25]

Dowie couldn't contain himself and blurted out, "No sir!" Alexander looked with surprise at the young man with the impassioned face and shining eyes, and the class sat on tenterhooks to see what would happen next. Fortunately for Dowie, Dr Alexander was a gracious man and rose to the challenge. He asked, "Why? Why do you say that the gifts have not passed away?"

Dowie responded, "Because I was healed when dying. 'The gifts and the calling of God are without repentance.' Not one of these gifts has passed away."

"Well," he replied. "Mr Dowie, write a thesis, put in your caveat. We shall be glad to hear you."[26] Dowie did just that, and Alexander had the privilege of hearing the first Dowie sermon on divine healing. According to Dowie, "no one put up an argument against him."[27] He later wrote, "I fought my fight in that College, with one of the best men that ever lived, who had tried to mislead, knowing no better."[28]

A DREAM IS BORN

Dowie seldom, if ever, acknowledged dependency upon anyone

for his theological views.[29]   However, he was in contact with several people at this time whose theology may well have influenced his later ministry, particularly in the areas of social reform and eschatology.

His friend Thomas Guthrie was an outstanding social reformer whose *Ragged Schools* for impoverished children saw the percentage of children imprisoned in Edinburgh fall from 5% to only 1% in only four years.

Guthrie took a holistic view of ministry and for him,

> ...to change the face of a district required, in his opinion, a more extensive and efficient system of cultivation - a school for children; a church with its door open to the poorest of the inhabitants; and a large staff of zealous men and women - each with their own section of families to visit and all working in harmony, like bees in a hive, under the direction of the minister, their captain, bishop or superintendent.[30]

Guthrie's contemporary Thomas Chalmers was another pioneering social reformer. Although Chalmers passed away in 1847, as the spiritual architect of the Free Church, he radically changed the spiritual dynamic of Scotland. For Chalmers religion was not a 'me and mine' activity, but rather for the benefit of the whole community. It was said he always had "a Utopia" in his sights, and that he could not "separate the social for the personal, the general for the particular, the temporal for the spiritual."[31]

When Chalmers died, his mantle as the father figure of the

Free Church fell to Robert Smith Candlish, Principal of the Free Church College. Dowie described Candlish as "one of Scotland's greatest men,"[32] and part of "a mighty company of wonderful men"[33] from an earlier generation.

This "mighty company" were young ministers and theology students when Irving was in his heydey and, after Irving's death, his influence lived on through them. As a young student, Candlish knew Irving personally, enjoyed his "ministrations" and became a supporter of Irving's end-time views.[34]

Irving's inspiration came through when Candlish later wrote about "the primitive and apostolic" church that God would raise up in the last days.[35] The conversion of the Jews was intimately bound up with the future glory of the true church because, "when the Lord built up Zion, he would return in glory."[36]

These beliefs inspired him to propose and secure the first mission of the modern church to the Jewish people - *Mission of Inquiry to the Jews*,[37] when in 1839 four Church of Scotland ministers - Robert Murray McCheyne, Dr Alexander Black, Dr Alexander Keith and Andrew Bonar - left for Palestine.

Andrew and Horatius Bonar were also active in the Scottish church during Dowie's time in Edinburgh and part of that earlier group impacted by Irving. The brothers were hugely influential in promoting pre-millennialism and the prophetic place of the Jews in God's end-time plans.[38]

Interestingly, Horatius Bonar believed that an Elijah figure would arise before the Second Coming of Christ, writing, "Elijah will be his forerunner at his second coming to judge an unbelieving world."[39]

In 1870 Bonar went on to publish "The Jew" in the *Quarterly Prophetic Journals* and expressed the view that,

> ...all human calculations as to the earth's future – political or scientific, philosophical or religious – must fail if they do not take into account God's great purpose regarding the standing of Israel at the Last Day... This is the day of the election; the age of the glory will follow...[40]

And lastly, Professor John Duncan is worthy of mention, according to Dowie, "the greatest scholar in Edinburgh" (in Greek and Hebrew).[41] A former missionary to the Jews in Hungary, Duncan's passion for the Jewish people was such he held the honorary title 'Rabbi' Duncan.

These figures are important because, significantly, Dowie received his first vision of Zion when a student in Edinburgh,

> I was riding through the parks when a sudden fog came down. As I looked the sun flashed out suddenly and there as if resting on the edge of the world, I saw the golden spires and outline of the city that had been with me in my dreams.[42]

Although his ideas would develop over the years, the seed thoughts were evidently there, even at this early stage. Dowie expected a new society to come out of a move of the Holy Spirit. His brave new world would be more than inner transformation; it would change the very fabric of society.

And most important of all – it would prepare the way for the Second Coming of the Lord.

THE DEVIL HAS HIS WAY

Dreams are all very well, but they don't pay the bills. In the summer of 1871, events took a turn for the worst that brought Dowie's studies to an end and put his dream of a golden city on hold for three decades.

A cablegram arrived with the grim news that John Murray was in financial trouble. No more money would be sent, and Dowie should return forthwith.

Dowie was devastated. His "beloved Scotland" was calling for him to help. God was calling for him to help.[43] But others needed help too. His own flesh and blood. He decided to go back to Australia, a decision he would bitterly regret,

> We once allowed the Devil to trick us in Edinburgh, Scotland and to turn us away twenty-nine years ago from plans which would long since have led to the establishment of the Christian Catholic Church in Zion. [44]

Back in Adelaide, Dowie worked as a clerk for two years in an ironmonger's store, a time he described melodramatically as "great darkness."[45] Was his dream of a golden city over before it had even begun?

God had a bigger plan for Dowie than he could have ever imagined. All things come at their proper time, and John Murray used his contacts to secure Dowie's ordination into the Congregational Union and on 25 May 1872, appointed to Alma, sixty miles from Adelaide.[46] A new chapter was about to begin.

3 PASTOR DOWIE

Dowie in Alma

*"I have spread my dreams beneath your feet. Tread softly
because you tread on my dreams."*
W.B. Yeats

EVERYBODY NEEDS TO START somewhere - but the brave
new day proved a slow burner. Alma was a little country
pastorate, covering ninety square miles and with four preaching
stations. The travelling wore him out - the apathy finished him
off.

Letters home to his parents tell of his frustration with the
congregation and their unwillingness to move forward. In

Edinburgh, he worked alongside people who were on fire for God, ministering to crowds of troubled, lost souls. He could "take an old street pulpit and fill the streets," as far as the eye could see.[1] A thousand people would gather to hear him preach, but now the population was hardly that in the whole ninety square mile parish!

And so, only six months into the job, Dowie sat alone in his little room at his wits' end. The dull headache which began hours before seemed to intensify in the silence, as he looked despairingly at the church accounts spread out before him. Thirty-six pounds in six months! Combined with the grant from the denomination, it didn't even cover his expenses.[2]

He groaned when he recalled only six people were in his last meeting. To compound matters, the church leadership were so far from God; it was impossible to turn the situation around. Dowie decided it would be "utter ruin" to delay the inevitable.[3] Worn out emotionally and physically, wearily he put pen to paper,

> After much prayer and consideration for the Divine guidance, I have determined to relinquish my office as your Pastor and now, therefore, resign it into your hands. I propose this to take effect on the Sabbath, December 29th...[4]

With his decision made, Dowie put out the lamp and went to bed. His times were in God's hands.

BACK HOME AGAIN

No word came from Heaven, and in the absence of any other

45

plan, Dowie went back to his parents' home. He would need to wait until late 1873 when another post became available in Manly Beach, Sydney. He threw himself into ministry in Manly with encouraging results. From an initial congregation of only twenty, soon there were seventy people in the Sunday school and full Sunday services.

It was a promising start but not enough. The corruption in Sydney sickened Dowie - "a terrible flood of moral evil" while in the midst of it, "men are discussing mere externals in religious matters."[5] There was a longing deep in his spirit for something better. He was tired of religion and weary of the corruption in the world. People were baptised into the church but with no real change to their lives. How could that be? Where was the fruit? He poured his heart out to a friend,

> There must be, for the whole Church of God, a more thorough belief in the presence and power of the Holy Spirit—and no doctrine and fact is at present less prominent than a simple reliance upon the Holy Spirit.[6]

For Dowie only "the baptism of the Holy Ghost" could create the kind of society where liberty would flourish in "true and faithful Christ-like communism in material things."[7]

At that time, his faith for divine healing was still in its infancy, yet there nonetheless. When his parents wrote to tell him of a man whose illness was incurable, he responded that he would write to him but to let the man know, "There is One 'who healeth all our diseases' who he knows can most effectually cheer him and on him doubtless he trusts."[8]

Dowie was on a journey. Though frustrated, his heart was open and not trussed-up with religion; rather he carried a God-given dissatisfaction in his spirit. It was a good, though painful, place to be.

I DREAM OF JEANIE

While Dowie fretted over the state of Sydney, the congregation did what congregations do. They fretted over the state of their pastor.

Much to their chagrin, Dowie was still single. This sorry situation despite the best efforts of the matrons in the group, who tried to get him paired up with several young women in succession. It was a nightmare. Literally! He confided in his mother his disturbed dreams of tea-meetings when plates and saucers took legs and charged him with teaspoons. Cakes and buns rained down on him and "a chorus of mammas and maidens pouted and cried 'Shame' in fashionable, musical discord."[9]

His misery was like Aesop's frogs, crying out to the boys stoning them, "What is fun to you, is death to us!"[10] Secretly, Dowie thought that he should marry. But how could he, when his heart was not his to give? For Dowie was already in love with his cousin Jeanie, daughter of the formidable Uncle Alexander. He just hadn't plucked up the courage to tell her yet - or him either, for that matter!

It was more than just trepidation at how Alexander would take it. Although ordinarily decisive, Dowie found himself at a loss to know how to broach the subject with Jeanie. He could weep for the sin around him. Rage at the apathy of the church.

But to tell the girl he loved what was in his heart - that was a different thing.

Dowie seldom cut himself any slack where emotion was concerned. There was right, and there was wrong. Emotion tended to get in the way of seeing things with the clarity required.

Jeanie Dowie

A breakthrough came when his overriding (but often self-imposed) sense of duty to point out other people's faults came to the rescue. Jeanie made plans to attend 'Hennings Ball', and Dowie felt it incumbent on him to write and discourage her from going. He inadvertently "let the cat out of the bag" when he told Jeanie his feelings for her went deeper than those of a cousin.[11]

Alas for poor Dowie, Jeanie was unimpressed and said so.[12] It would be another three years before he opened his heart to her again.

WEARYING IN WELL-DOING

The position in Manly didn't last. Dowie was torn between a desire to be in 'the team' (for him, the Congregational Church), or move in his gifting as an evangelist. From the promising start, a sudden catastrophic drop occurred in his opinion of the congregation,

> Church going there is but a perfect malaria of
> spiritual disease with it, slow fevers of indifference

and cowardice, leprosies of pride, hatred and vanity, burning fevers of money and pleasure seeking and an epidemic of vice.[13]

Faced with such depravity, he wanted to cry out, but God shut his mouth - "almost literally - my mouth is shut. God has his time I know, but I am tempted much to weary for its manifestation."[14]

God saw Dowie in his misery and his time in Manly was not in vain. One evening in 1874 as he hurried home, a young man penniless and begging, cried out to him. On hearing the Scottish lilt coming from the stranger, Dowie stopped. He gave him a few coins for a bed for the night and asked the young man to come back the next day.

When they met again, Dowie was amazed to find his visitor was the youngest son of Robert Smith Candlish, Principal of the Free College in Edinburgh. Candlish had recently died, and Dowie read his obituary in the Australian newspapers only a few days before.[15] Now here was his son sitting before him in an awful state.

John Candlish told Dowie that he came to Australia to build a new life. He planned to go and live with Dr Cairns, an old friend of his father. But his life fell apart when he fell into the wrong company and went back to his old ways, drinking too much and losing all his money and possessions.

"Do you know your father is dead?" Dowie gently asked. John started to weep, "Yes, I killed him."

Dowie's heart went out to him. "We will have a fight with the

Devil for you, son of many prayers. I shall ask God to answer them and help you all I can."[16] The young man recommitted his life to the Lord. After a few weeks, when Dowie was sure of John's change of heart, he wrote to Candlish's widow in Edinburgh to say her son was safe and now following God. Mrs Candlish in gratitude sent Dowie a copy of her husband's memoirs and movingly told him her husband's last words were, "Oh God, save my son. Save John."[17]

This was a telling moment in Dowie's life and shows the measure of the man he was at that time. Through the encounter with John Candlish, he became friends with Dr Cairns, another Free Church stalwart, who lived in Australia due to poor health. Cairns took a fatherly interest in Dowie and prophetically told him,

> Oh, I love you. Young man, I often think of what a fight you are going to have. The fights we have had are nothing to it. You are going to have a great fight.[18]

Dowie loved Dr Cairns. He loved anyone who loved the Lord with passion and abandon. These were the people that he associated with and those he wanted to help. It is too easy to look at the last years of Dowie's life, tragic though they were, and think these define John Alexander Dowie. They don't. He was a proud and noble evangelist. A helper of men. A helper who went all out to find the lost sons and daughters of the Kingdom and bring them home.

But Manly church was not right for him. Their vision was too small, too introspective for a man like Dowie. He needed to move on, that much he knew. The question was - where?

NEWTOWN

For a while, Dowie toyed with the idea of a return to Scotland.[19] Jeanie didn't want him; Manly wasn't for him. Perhaps he could go back and pick up where he left off with the Carrubbers Mission?

Those plans changed abruptly when a position came up in King Street, Newtown.[20] It was the largest Congregational church in New South Wales, with around a hundred and twenty members and seating for up to a thousand. The church served the professors and students of Camden College, the only theological seminary of the Congregationalists in Australia.

It seemed perfect, Dowie wrote to a friend to build, "a many-sided ministry."[21] When offered the post, he immediately accepted, staying on in Manly only to see the new church building completed. He took up his new charge in February 1875, and after the wilderness years, Dowie thought he had arrived. An impressive two-storey manse came with the post, which he furnished "in keeping with his new status."[22]

For their part, the congregation were delighted with their new pastor, with his preaching ability described as "extraordinary."[23] Furnishing his new home put him in debt - but no matter, he told a friend, it was important to give the right impression with his new position in the community.[24]

Unfortunately the step-up the property ladder proved a fly in the ointment, as it made Dowie even more acutely aware he was still a single man, rattling around in his big house. Help was at hand for Dowie's lonely heart when news arrived unexpectedly from his parents saying some guests were coming to visit from

Adelaide. A telegram followed soon after from his brother Andrew saying his guests were on route and could he go to meet them?[25]

Jeanie was coming to see him!

Dowie didn't know whether to be happy or sad. What could it mean? Maybe she had changed her mind? He dared not get his hopes up, he told himself sternly, as he frantically tried to get the creases out of his good shirt. The 'letter' was best forgotten.

LOVE AT LAST

She arrived with Uncle Alexander. After an awkward start, Dowie resolved to make their stay as pleasant as possible and played the part of the model host.

On the night before they left, Alexander, tired from the day's exertions, took himself off to bed. Finally left alone with Dowie, Jeanie got down to business. Inexperienced as he was in affairs of the heart, Dowie told his parents their conversation was entirely without "premeditation" on both their parts. But to his delight, Jeanie said she probably could love him! And he had been right all along about Hennings Ball.[26] It wasn't really for her.

Yet, she told him sadly, they were cousins, so how could they marry? Jeanie was clearly on more than a sight-seeing tour. She let herself be 'persuaded' that nothing in Scripture stood against them marrying. But there was still the thorny matter of Alexander. She had told her father about Dowie's letter, and he wasn't at all happy about the matter.[27] She pleaded with Dowie not to speak to him about marriage, as it would cause a fight.

With all other avenues of attack cut off, Dowie decided to call for reinforcements. He dispatched a letter to his parents, commissioning John Murray as his "ambassador" to Alexander.[28]

4 MARY

Newtown Church

. "Anybody can pray but what is the use of praying if you do not get results?"
John Alexander Dowie

WITH BOTH HIS DAUGHTER and now his brother in favour of a wedding, Alexander reluctantly conceded defeat and agreed to Jeanie marrying Dowie.

Doubtless, the manse with its impressive new furniture proved a factor in winning him over. That was short-lived. Over the years to follow, Alexander's relationship with his son-in-law went from barely disguised contempt to outright hostility. Dowie's feelings for his father-in-law followed a similar trajectory!

That was for a different day. For then, Dowie had enough battles to keep him occupied. As Jeanie made plans for their approaching wedding, he faced the biggest trial of his ministry to date. [1]

He had longed for a deeper baptism in the Holy Spirit. God answered that prayer by taking him to a situation that pushed him beyond anything he could deal with in his natural ability. Plague struck Newtown and Dowie went from one funeral to the next with a heavy heart, burying fifteen corpses in one day alone. Young men and women cut down in their prime, children dead before they had the chance to live.

Helplessness in the face of the onslaught created a tide of anger that threatened to overwhelm him.

The interior of Newtown Church

For some time he had warned the affluent congregation that the city's failure to dig a proper drainage system would lead to trouble. They thought it would only affect the poor. But he told them the same sickness that killed the poor would also take the lives of the rich.

Now it was too late, and death stalked the community. For Dowie, it was evident that greed and neglect caused this misery, not God. And despite all his warnings, he now had the awful distinction of being one of the only ministers left in the area to bury victims of the plague.

Dead children lay in homes, without father or mother to grieve over them. The eerie silence, where once peals of laughter rang out was almost worse than the cries of the sufferers still clinging to life.

THE WILL OF GOD

One day God turned it all around. The morning started pretty much the same as any other. Dowie pulled himself out of bed before dawn and set out to visit a home where the family were in a pitiful state. When he got there, the sight appalled him. A woman lay sick, with dead baby twins by her side. Her husband had abandoned her.

The human misery encapsulated in that one scene said it all. As Dowie stood with the stench of death in his nostrils, he thought of the lie he had heard so many times, "This is the will of God."

Swallowing the bile rising in his throat, half caused by the smell and the rest by the rage within, he searched the nearby houses and found a woman who would clean the house for half a sovereign. Another who, for a sovereign, brought out the pathetic little corpses and cleaned the bedding for the bereaved mother. With his grim duty done, Dowie walked home, overcome by despair and at a loss to know how to move forward.

A NEW DOCTRINE

Despite "much thinking and praying" he just didn't know how to get people to put their faith in God for their deliverance from the plague.

Frustrated with his inadequacy and depressed at the continuous sight of death, Dowie couldn't find any peace within. Divine healing was a new doctrine for his church. As their pastor, he felt he should be leading the way, yet it was not at all "plain" even to him at that time.

It was still early morning when he reached the door of his manse. His housekeeper took one look at his gaunt face and urged him to eat. She laid down breakfast, but it tasted like gravel. How could he eat with such misery around him?

He put on his coat again and left for yet more visits to sufferers. This time to a family from his own church. The mother was a helper at Newton Congregational and her three children, all in Dowie's Sunday school. Arnold was nine, Cecelia, eleven and Mary, fourteen. The children were sick and their lives uncertain, like so many others around them.

Dowie comforted the mother as best he could, then trudged wearily back to his manse. Time was getting on, and he had to change clothes for the afternoon task of burying yet more dead at Haslam's Creek Cemetery.

Sitting down in his study, he opened his Bible at his text for the following Sunday morning,

> Even Jesus of Nazareth, how that God anointed him with the Holy Spirit and with power, who went about doing good and healing all that were oppressed of the Devil, for God was with him (Acts 10:38).

The words turned over repeatedly in his mind, as a feeling of total despair washed over his soul. Perhaps he was not called by God at all. Was God not with him? And if God was with him, why did he not see miracles as the Bible promised?

Was Galilee any worse than the misery in Newtown?

Just then, the doorbell rang noisily. Dowie started violently.

His nerves were at breaking point. Was there never a moment when he could get just five minutes to himself! What now? The sound of hushed but urgent, voices drifted up from the lobby, followed by rapid steps on the stairs.

He looked up to see his housekeeper at the study door, breathless and with her eyes full of tears. "Oh, Mr Dowie," she blurted out. "Mary is dying!"

GOD'S WAYS

He ran from the study, without stopping for hat or coat, taking the stairs two at a time. The family lived only a short distance away, and he sprinted the length of it, with his long dark hair and beard flowing.

Storming into the house, he ran straight into the doctor. "Doctor," he said. "What are you doing here, anything?"

"Nothing," the doctor replied. "No one can help her; she is dying. Science has spoken the last word and has exhausted all remedies. Aren't God's ways marvellous?"

Dowie lunged at the man, as though he were the Devil incarnate. Grabbing him by the collar, he retorted, "Doctor, do not lie! This is not the work of God! Do you hear her? She is cursing, she is swearing! Mary had a clean heart and has it still. The Devil is controlling her tongue and her being. It is the Devil that has thrown her into that fit, making her bite her tongue until the blood comes. Don't you see it? Doctor?"

"No," he said. "I do not see it. Let me go! You are not moderate!"

"No," Dowie shouted back. "I am not moderate! I have been thinking all the morning that I was like a shepherd whose sheep and lambs were being torn by wolves. I see the teeth in their throats; I see the heart being torn out of them, I see them lying dead everywhere, I have been able to do nothing, but now I have a stick!"

The doctor looked at Dowie incredulously. "My God let me go before you hit me!"

"Never fear," Dowie replied. "I will be glad to let you go, but I have a stick! I do not know much about healing through faith in Jesus but I was healed years ago, and I am going to have it out with the Devil now. There is one thing that I am sure of - 'The Son of God was manifested that he might destroy the works of the Devil,' and this is the work of the Devil!"

The doctor quickly gathered his things and left. The man was mad!

THE VALLEY OF DEATH

Dowie went up to Mary, lying drenched in sweat and frothing blood and saliva. He knew this girl so well; she was like a daughter to him. Sweet, kind, holy, gentle, but this horror cursed and swore like a fiend!

In the corner of the room, Mary's mother was beside herself with grief, rocking herself back and forward. "Oh Pastor," she cried. "It is worse than death to hear her talk so."

Dowie responded sharply, "She is not speaking, that is the Devil. Now lock the door."

He knew this was the moment. He was going to have it out with the Enemy. "Now," he told Mary's mother, struggling to control his thinly-veiled anger. "Let's get down to business."

Rage at the suffering took Dowie to a place where respectable Christianity seldom ventured, the valley of death. A place where he would confront the powers of Hell, with the victory of the Cross. But there would be a battle, for Satan would not give in easily.

Many years later, Dowie preached on what happened to him that day,

> I was angry with Satan and sin and disease and death and Hell, and I am angry still. I do well to be angry! God is angry! Some of you people have not enough divine love to be angry with the Devil. I went down into the Valley. I think I have never been as deep in the Valley, before or since. Satan, Sin, Disease, Death and Hell were there. I began to pray...I told God that I believed that all these diseases that were sweeping off multitudes were the work of the Devil.

> I told my Father in Heaven that he had sent his Son to "destroy the works of the Devil." I told him that I was a minister of his and that if I could not be used to offer the Prayer of Faith that saved the sick, I would resign. It was my business, I said, to take care of the sheep, which he had given me.

> Then I went on and said, "And now I ask for this life. I plead that thou wilt destroy the Devil's work in her." I pleaded every promise that came to my mind and all

at once I said, "These signs shall follow them that believe. In my Name, they shall lay hands on the sick, and they shall recover."

"Lord," I prayed, "I never did it before, but I now lay my hands upon this girl and plead that she shall recover and recover now!"

All at once, the peace of God filled the room. Dowie fell silent.

SHE'S ALIVE!

He took Mary's long, black hair from across her face, spread it out on the pillow, then wiped away the perspiration and bloody froth from her mouth.

Mary was quite serene now, with her hands resting still by her sides. Her mother, almost afraid to speak, tearfully asked, "Is she dead?"

"Dead!" Dowie exclaimed. "No. Mary is alive! I've taken her pulse, and it is normal. There is no fever. We have been appealing to God to destroy the works of the Devil and to raise her, and he has answered."

As he checked her pulse again, Dowie realised in less than half an hour; he had to be on the train with the corpses destined for Haslam's Creek Cemetery. But he was loath to leave the atmosphere of peace and tranquillity. Though his eyes could see it, his mind struggled to take in the magnitude of what had just happened!

He called out to the maid, "Louise, bring in a cup of chocolate and some bread and butter. I will stay a little longer." After a few minutes, Dowie gently woke Mary. She slowly opened her eyes and smiled up at him.

"Pastor, when did you come? I have had such a long, beautiful sleep; I must have slept a long time!"

Dowie asked, "Are you well?"

"Yes," she answered, looking longingly at the hot chocolate and food.

"Hungry?"

"Very," she replied. "Oh, I am so hungry!"

He poured the chocolate and sat quietly watching as she gulped it down and ravenously ate the food. After a few minutes, Dowie roused himself and went to the next room where the other children Arnold and Cecelia both lay ill. After he prayed over the two younger children, they both also recovered.

From that day forward, the plague claimed no further victims in Dowie's church. It was a miraculous deliverance, born of desperation and through it, God had taught Dowie a truth that he would take to the nations.

That the same Jesus who went around "doing good and healing all that were oppressed of the Devil" is just the same today.

5 JEANIE AND DOWIE

The Clergyman

"A wife of noble character, who can find?"
Proverbs 31:10

JEANIE AND DOWIE MARRIED in the following month on 25 May 1876, at Stow Congregational Church in Adelaide. The bride was stunning - as all brides are - and the groom wore the little gold cufflinks that Mary, Arnold and Cecilia bought him in thanks for his prayers that saved their lives.[1] They settled into married life, with Dowie, the exemplary clergyman, although with every passing day, feeling more and more frustrated with the lackadaisical Christianity around him.

He was thoroughly sick of committees and church politics. Where was their desire for the Kingdom of God? Though he gave it his best shot, Dowie was never going to be satisfied with anything less than his dream of the golden city!

Jeanie soon fell pregnant and moved back to live with her family for support. That proved a mistake because, not long after their son Gladstone was born, marital strife had raised its head between Dowie and his wife.[2]

She confided in her parents Dowie was in debt when they married and now thinking of leaving the church in Newtown. With a new-born baby. Where would they go?

Alexander hit the roof and despatched an icy blast of correspondence to Dowie, reprimanding him for neglecting his first Christian duty to support his family. Dowie had nowhere to go, and Alexander was not happy with him dragging his daughter and grandchild with him![3]

Alexander Dowie

Dowie, outraged at his father-in-law's meddling, retorted to Jeanie that it was none of Alexander's business what he did. If he spent more money on books than his family, that was nothing to do with her father either.

He wasn't "a cobbler" like Alexander. It was an honest profession, yet couldn't be compared with his ministry. Books were the tools of his trade![4]

He told her sharply, "I won't have you destroy my life. I married a 'helpmeet' not a hinderer."[5]

Anyway, he told Jeanie, it was all over now. He offered his resignation at the Deacons' meeting on the previous evening, and they accepted, so that put an end to it. It was nothing to do with her or her father.

As to having nowhere to go, a deputation from Waterloo Church had already approached him to take another post. When he refused, they applauded his reasons for leaving the Congregational church.[6]

According to Dowie, the Congregational Union was hopelessly corrupt, with "Mammon" the President, and "Cliques" the standing committee to oversee the day-to-day running.[7] He was tired of it all and had decided to set up his own Free Christian Church.

Jeanie would just have to live with it or go her own way. She wasn't the woman he thought her when they married. And the cruellest cut of all for Jeanie. If only he could get back the money he spent in marrying her, then he wouldn't owe anyone anything![8]

If Dowie had been a little more conciliatory, he might have saved them both a lot of heartache. Jeanie was insecure, and the gossips in Newtown had filled her head with all sorts of stories about her husband.[9]

65

But the acrimonious correspondence revealed an ugly side to the man Jeanie married. Willing to lay down everything for his calling, unwilling to show grace when any opposition followed. He lashed out at the criticism and summarily told Jeanie she was dispensable. If she was not for him, she was against him, in which case he had no interest in her.

In the event of Jeanie's refusal to go to Sydney, Dowie told her he "may feel it is his duty" to go to London.[10] It was up to her whether she came or not. Much as he missed his son, he would rather the boy died in infancy than grew up in a broken family, where Jeanie would not support him.[11]

Harsh and cruel words, even when spoken in anger.

MOVING ON

After much pen and ink spilt in the lover's tiff, Jeanie acquiesced to go back to Dowie. The correspondence had spiralled downwards, with Dowie telling her she was spiritually "self-divorced."[12] But her "three nice letters" healed the rift and he was magnanimously prepared to forgive and move on.[13]

A first publishing venture in 1877 *Rome's Polluted Springs*, opened with what would be Dowie's signature statement in the years to come,

> I represent no party, no church organisation and no formulated creed and for my utterances here this evening no one is responsible but myself—and I deeply feel the weight of that responsibility, for I am accountable to God.[14]

True to his word, he left the Congregational Church in 1878, dramatically appearing on his last day with a glass of wine and announcing to the congregation, "These be thy gods O Israel!"[15]

The poor old dears in Newtown must have taken quite a turn. Where did that nice young man go, who joined only a few years before? Some said his mind was going.[16]

Dowie was unrepentant and sold his expensive furniture to fund evangelistic outreaches in the Royal Theatre in Sydney, meeting with remarkable success. Within only four weeks, over a thousand people gathered to hear him preach.[17] Another publication followed in 1879, with two lectures, delivered at the Victoria Theatre, published under the title *The Drama, the Press and the Pulpit.*

He was unashamedly open for business and beholden to no one except God. He now believed it was unethical for a minister to be dependent upon his church for a salary. Alexander was no doubt relieved to hear that Dowie's scruples in these matters only went so far. The new group guaranteed him a weekly income of fifteen pounds - seven pounds for expenses and eight pounds for Dowie.[18] By no means a fortune but enough when supplemented by his parents who sent him new clothes to preach in.[19]

However, the overheads proved more costly than anticipated. Offerings did not bring in enough to cover the rent for the Royal Theatre, and the group were forced to move to progressively smaller buildings – first the Protestant Hall and then the Masonic Hall.[20] Undaunted, Dowie pointed affectionately to his group of several hundred "loyal and devoted people," most of whom were converted through his ministry.[21]

Though these were hard times, Dowie's grit and determination saw him through. His father-in-law mocked that God did not do miracles to feed minister's wives and children.[22] The Chairman of the Congregational Union said he didn't have what it took to go it alone.[23] His possessions were gone but in their place lay a greater prize, souls won for the Kingdom of God.[24] He would rather go outside the camp than "fill the pastorate of the fattest, sleepiest and most complacent church of the Laodiceans."[25]

Dowie's confidence in his calling was unshakeable. If the churches would not evangelise, he would, and by every means at his disposal. He wrote and published twenty tracts, distributing over two hundred thousand copies in Sydney.[26]

One pastor who indignantly complained of Dowie's evangelism in his area, received a letter back, caustically telling him,

> I consider your judgment to be as feeble and incapable as your ministry; I do not reckon it to be of the slightest value…I wish I knew who distributed these 'obnoxious tracts' among your flock; I would certainly commend his choice of a field.[27]

His passion for reaching the lost was all-consuming. It outweighed any need for diplomacy. He was John Alexander, a helper of men. The other churches could join him, or get out of the way - he wasn't stopping.

THE POLITICIAN

Although his zeal was commendable, even at this early stage, the fault lines in Dowie's personality were beginning to show. His self-belief was dizzying. The need was all around him, and the need was now. So why wait any longer?

The East Sydney parliamentary seat came up in a by-election, and some friends persuaded him to stand for Parliament on a temperance platform. Dowie jumped at the chance, pushing all thoughts of the mission aside. He campaigned enthusiastically against denominational schools and for fairer land ownership, fewer alcohol licences, better public services and taxation reform.[28]

But Dowie was not a popular figure. His publishing ventures and evangelism had convinced many that he was a firebrand and an agitator. Powerful forces arraigned against him and on the day of the polls, the promised support did not materialise.

When the votes were counted, he came in a poor third, with only a hundred and forty-seven votes.[29] Incensed at the public humiliation, Dowie maintained he was sacrificed, not defeated.[30] His response to a letter attacking him in the press showed a growing anger at criticism that he neglected his mission work for an unsuccessful political campaign.

He was, "no more disposed to write failure on his ministry than brand Paul, John Bunyan, or John Wesley as 'failures' because they cared more for the souls of Christ's sheep than for their golden fleeces."[31]

The obvious flaw in the argument is the Apostle Paul, John Bunyan and John Wesley did not give up evangelism for politics. In Dowie's world, there was only one way of doing things – his way. This tendency to lash out when criticised was an unfortunate weakness of his personality. Jeanie had experienced it, now these public spats with his critics did him no credit.

Would he have changed if he had known this behaviour would see him die alone and friendless? Probably not. Still, the failed political foray showed how easily distracted Dowie could be by a new project and how staunchly he would fight his corner, rather than just admit he was wrong.

THE STING

In the post-election aftermath, Dowie was not in a good place – spiritually or financially. By turning his attention to politics, numbers had fallen away from his mission.[32]

Negotiations with his mission committee saw him offer to reduce his salary to six pounds weekly. The board responded that offerings barely brought that in, and they could not give the guarantee he wanted.[33]

The outlook was bleak and the Heavens as brass. Suddenly, a last-minute reprieve when the committee promised a salary of five pounds weekly for Dowie's personal expenses.[34] They would meet in the International Hall. It was small but enough to get back on track until the numbers picked up.

Dowie should have grasped the lifeline from Heaven with both hands. Unfortunately, he was too busy nursing a chronic case of bruised pride. He had failed - and failed publicly. Two things that inevitably led to bad decision-making on his part.

Conman George Holding watched events from the wings, carrying a letter of introduction from Dowie's father. On the face of it, Holding presented himself as a very wealthy man, claiming large estates back in England. He told Dowie he wanted to help him and promised twenty-one thousand pounds upfront and to leave Dowie his entire fortune of two hundred thousand pounds in his will.[35]

From five pounds a week to a fortune! It sounded too good to be true! The church committee thought so at any rate. They were uneasy and began to make their own inquiries about the mysterious Mr Holding.[36]

Disregarding the advice of well-meaning friends, Dowie made plans to stand *again* for Parliament in South Sydney, with Holding's money bankrolling the campaign.[37] Meanwhile, Holding set off for England, allegedly to wind up his estates, and with three hundred pounds of Dowie's borrowed money.[38]

> **Dowie and his Tabernacle.**
>
> Mr. Holding. who promised the Rev. Dowie £20,000 for his synagogue in Sydney, as been arrested in Melbourne on a charge f obtaining £300 upon false representations from the Rev. Mr. Dowie.
>
> Newcastle Morning Herald, 8 Jan 1886

Everyone told Dowie to be careful, not least his father. But Dowie stormed back that John Murray was conspiring to get his own hands on Holding's money.[39]

When Holding didn't return, the awful realisation finally hit Dowie that he had been conned. To make matters worse, rumours circulated he had received a large sum of money from Holding and kept it for himself.[40]

If things were bad before, this was an unmitigated disaster. Holding later turned up in Melbourne, impersonating a Salvation Army officer and confessed to duping Dowie out of his money.

However, by that time the damage was done.[41]   The mission committee resigned and their five pounds a week went with them.   With his backers gone, Dowie left Sydney in December 1880, saddled with yet more debt.

Before he left, he promised his last remaining supporters they would hear of him again when he inaugurated one of the grandest religious movements the world had ever seen![42]

In that, he was undoubtedly correct - they certainly heard about him.   But his creditors had to wait until 1901 when Overseer Voliva arrived and paid off Dowie's long-standing debts, racked up during the Holding fiasco.[43] Dowie then visited in 1904 with his entourage and exclaimed, "Why the place seems to have shrunk!" He went on to tell the Australians they were "full of conceit" and did not realise how "small" they were.[44]

If Dowie accumulated enemies as quickly as he accumulated debt, there were undoubtedly some occasions when he brought it on himself.   Throughout his ministry, supporters loaned him money to finance his plans. Yet financial propriety was hardly a high point – an unfortunate trait, given the millions that would flow through his hands in the years to come.

FAILED AGAIN

At the beginning of the 1880s, he would have been glad of a decent meal, never mind a fortune. Jeanie went back to her parents, as the family were now without a regular income.

With his credibility at an all-time low, in his frustration, Dowie wanted to fight everyone. A temporary position with the Salvation Army saw him fall out with the local Salvation Army

Captain and form a rival group. To compound matters, he took the Commissioner of Police to court for obstructing a procession, only for the judge to throw the case out. Dowie paid the costs.[45] Another failed court battle followed with a leading spiritualist, Thomas Walker. Dowie again paid his costs.[46]

His letter of 29 March 1882, sent to Jeanie from temporary lodgings, revealed the depth of his misery, yet his earnest hope that God would turn it all around,

> Once more, I have to write you the discouraging word 'failed.' But I live, and God lives, and it cannot be that the night will long endure and that one who strives to do his will shall always fail.[47]

His heart was in the right place, if not his head. Dowie had something special in him. The fire in his bones never left him. Although he seemed to stagger aimlessly from one fight to the next, God was still with him.

SACKVILLE STREET

God's ways are at times baffling to us. In fact, we might question if they are his 'ways' at all, or rather the redeeming grace he showers upon our lives and makes straight the things that are crooked.

In Dowie's next post he didn't just get it wrong, he hit a new personal best. It was a brief period of cover at Sackville Street Tabernacle to give the Reverend Cherbury a sabbatical.

Things turned sour when Dowie didn't agree with the use of the church by non-converted temperance speakers. When the existing office bearers told him it was none of his business, he tried to sack them.

Cherbury made a hasty return from London when letters told him of Dowie as "a regular persecuting society of the Church."[48] A church split then loomed when Dowie next tried to sack Reverend Cherbury, under the terms of a Trust Deed he implemented in Cherbury's absence.

To be fair to Dowie, he claimed the church grew under his leadership, and many supported him in wanting reform. It is clear though from Dowie's own account when Cherbury returned Dowie did not "immediately retire from the pulpit."[49]

A lengthy publication followed to tell Dowie's side of the story, *Sin in the Camp – A Vindication of the Character of John Alexander Dowie.*

A vindication of your character, running to no less than a hundred and eighteen pages, is never going to make for inspiring reading. True to form, it is a rather dismal publication. But it does give the story of Sackville Street, as seen through the eyes of Dowie.

In his mind, he was the embattled Servant of God, standing against the Goliath of the Philistines, the hapless Reverend Cherbury. Dowie called a special meeting on 11 February 1883 to seek a vote of no confidence in Cherbury.[50] It turned into what Dowie described as, "a disgraceful riot." When the majority of the church refused to back him, Dowie left the church, pelted with earth, and to the backdrop of a woman screaming, "I'll kill him!"[51]

Can anything good come out of the Sackville Street saga?
Actually, yes. Well for Dowie at any rate. When he left, ninety-
nine members of Cherbury's congregation went with him. Two
weeks later, they formed the Free Christian Church of Fitzroy,
with Dowie as their leader preaching on divine healing.[52]

6 SIGNS AND WONDERS

Dowie with the Fitzroy marchers

"I will show wonders in the Heavens above and signs on the earth below."

Acts 2:19

DOWIE HAD PROVED MORE of a blunt instrument than a polished arrow. Yet the same God who raised up Pharaoh for his purpose, could take a John Alexander Dowie and use him likewise.

Until then, Dowie created a lot of heat but not a lot of light. But around this time things began to change. Battles with spiritualists convinced him that spiritualism was no more than the diabolic counterfeit to the gifts of the Spirit. God gave his

"Apostolic Church" power over the Devil at Pentecost, and he never withdrew that power.[1] Its purpose was to equip the church for "the Great Warfare" against the forces of darkness.[2]

Dowie was now more than ready to move in that anointing. He was sick of watching the works of the Devil glorified in the church as "the will of God"!

THE FREE CHRISTIAN CHURCH

The Free Christian Church met in the local town hall, with divine healing at the forefront of Dowie's message. Stories of "Modern Miracles" rapidly circulated Fitzroy and people began to crowd into the services to see for themselves.[3]

"Modern miracles" were met with some scepticism by the press. One journalist asked for proof. Dowie sent him to meet Mrs Coats of 42 Westgarth Street, Fitzroy. She testified that in March 1883, her friends called for Dowie when it appeared she would not survive the night.

He asked her, "Can you say, 'Bless the Lord, oh my soul, who forgiveth all mine iniquities?'"

"Yes," she told him.

"Why can't you finish it?" he asked. 'Who healeth all my disease'?"

"How can I?" she cried despondently. "And who will look after my poor babies when I am gone?" In her despair, Mrs Coats grasped "at the hope held out" and received immediate healing.[4]

Lucy Parker and her son

Lucy Parker of Moor Street, Fitzroy was next on the list. Lucy testified she went to Dowie for prayer in July 1883, suffering from cancer in her eye. After Dowie had prayed, the cancer burst and flowed out. Lucy was pregnant at the time and her baby born in perfect health.[5]

Mrs Carpenter, of Charles Street, Fitzroy suffered from partial deafness for fourteen years. One evening, she sat near the front of the Fitzroy Town Hall, straining to hear Dowie sing the words,

> *She only touched the hem of his garment*
> *As to his side, she stole*
> *Amid the crowd that gathered around him*
> *And straightway she was made whole.*

She reached out in faith, and God miraculously restored her hearing. Mrs Kerr of Rupert Street, Collingwood received household healing. She testified to deliverance from asthma, leg problems and seventeen 'cauliflower' skin cancers; her husband of typhoid fever and their daughter of a lifelong spinal complaint.

Rebecca Maynard of Hanover Street, Fitzroy had her sight totally restored after seven years blindness in her left eye. A witness to Rebecca's healing said,

> I sat by her side for some hours waiting her turn and talked with her. Her eye seemed withered up. I saw her afterwards, on coming out, with it open and clear![6]

Catherine Caraes of Napier-Street, received healing from total blindness of twelve years standing. She sat in Dowie's home listening to an address on 'Healing by Faith' and "suddenly grasped the idea." She sprang up, crying out, "Oh, I can see! The Lord hath healed me!"[7]

These were powerful testimonies for the people of Fitzroy. Not a story of something, that happened somewhere, to somebody – but rather miracles going on in their town, to people they knew!

'DR' CHRIST

In May 1884, the *Port Adelaide News* reported a revival of faith healing through the ministries of evangelist John Alexander Dowie and spiritualist George Milner Stephen. "Numerous" people, personally known to the writer, had received healing.

For the writer, the difference between Dowie and the spiritualists was primarily around how they exercised healing power. The spiritualists maintained power emanated from their spirit and left them exhausted after ministering to a sufferer. By way of contrast,

> Mr Dowie asserts that no force leaves his body when he performs a cure – that he devotes twenty out of every twenty-four hours to healing the sick…It is 'Dr' Christ who does the healing, and it is asserted there is not a sick person in Dowie's congregation.[8]

'Dr Christ' later changed to 'Dr Dowie', but throughout his healing ministry, Dowie emphasised Christ did the healing, not him.[9] And as the report noted, his healing message was radically different from that of the spiritualists. It was so simple that even a child could take hold of it. The Devil was bad, and God was good. Christ's mission was to destroy the work of the Evil One. He succeeded in that mission, and therefore healing was part of the Atonement.[10]

THE 'SMOTING' ANGEL

It was just too simple for some people. A healing mission to Ballarat provoked a disgruntled resident to complain to the local newspaper that Dowie attributed all sickness to the Devil. The writer argued Dowie did not take into account, "God's afflictive dispensations" whereby, "the Angel of the Lord smote" people in their sin.[11]

The sick were deserving of "the utmost sympathy from every conscientious and upright Christian," not charlatans like Dowie![12]

Such voices were relatively few. In defiance of the alleged 'Smoting' Angel, the Ballarat sick turned out in their hundreds to hear the message of divine healing. In one meeting, Dowie asked the crowd to raise their hands if they believed in divine healing. Four hundred people agreed, bar only two dissenters.[13]

After years of struggling, things began to move fast in his ministry. The healing anointing gave him a new authority, and people flocked to hear him preach.

Alongside that, Dowie was also experiencing his own inner transformation. Just before the Ballarat mission, a mysterious blue light appeared in his bedroom that separated into four flames, then burst into many "tongues of fire."[14] He called out to

Jeanie, who came running into the room. She was initially fearful. What could it mean?

They didn't have too long to wait before finding out. Shortly after that evening, an invitation arrived from Holiness preacher William Boardman to speak at the London *International Conference on Divine Healing and True Holiness*, in the summer of 1885.

Boardman's letter confirmed what was growing in Dowie's heart. God was calling him to move out in his ministry. To take his gospel of divine healing to the nations.

But the timing of the invitation seemed wrong! There was still so much to do in Fitzroy! Dowie carefully penned his response telling Boardman he could not attend because "the Lord hath need of me at this juncture in this outpost of the field."

He went on,

> All over the world, there are signs that "the old time religion" is returning to its primitive lines of spiritual power and that, despite the forces of an organised and widespread formalism, true Christians are everywhere realising that "the Spirit giveth Life." Amongst these signs, the revival of faith in Jesus as the Healer and the perpetuity of the gifts of Healing by the Holy Spirit are occupying a most important place.[15]

Dowie told Boardman he intended to minister worldwide in three years' time, beginning in America and then moving on to Europe. In the meantime, he would continue to work in

Australia and planned to launch a weekly publication dedicated to divine healing.

ETERNITIES OVER US

That settled it. Well, for a couple of hours anyway. By evening, doubt had crept into his mind. The Conference was a prestigious gathering. Would another invitation come? He needed to hear from God.

As everyone slept, Dowie climbed a hill, high above the city, with the canopy of the Heavens over his head. Gazing up at the night sky, he asked the Lord if it was a mistake to turn down Boardman's invitation. All was silent, as Dowie searched the sky for some trace of the invisible God. Goethe's haunting words echoed through his mind,

> *Veiled, the dark Portal*
> *Goal of all mortal*
> *Stars silent rest o'er us*
> *Graves under us silent.*[16]

Then suddenly a shift and Dowie was in the Spirit. The ground seemed to rise up around him, wailing in pain from all corners of the globe. He threw himself to the ground in an agony of despair. Was there no help for the suffering millions? Lifting up his eyes, he scanned the Heavens, desperately seeking some token of divine favour. The majesty of the night sky overwhelmed until the "comfort of a divine peace" filled his heart,

> And as I looked I knew that I, too, had to carry the
> Cross of Christ from land to land and bid a sin-

stricken and disease smitten world to see that the Christ who died on Calvary had made atonement for sickness as well as for sin, that with his stripes.[17]

That was the answer he needed. Dowie turned for home. He would take his gospel of divine healing to the nations, in God's way, and in God's time.

JOHNSTONE STREET TABERNACLE

Thoughts of world mission put aside; he threw himself into ministry in the Free Christian Church in Fitzroy. With a growing congregation, they needed a place to call home. Never one to let the grass grow under his feet, Dowie raised enough money to build a church and one of the congregation offered up favourable terms to lease some land with an option to buy.

The Johnstone Street Tabernacle opened on 3 August 1884, with seating for an impressive three thousand people. Every week the hall was packed and bursting with testimonies to the healing power of God.

Jeanie Dowie recalled her husband in these early days as moving in, "the fire of the Methodists, the water of the Baptists, the stability of the Presbyterians and the ablest of the church governments of Congregationalists, taking that which he counted good from them all.[18]

It must have been a remarkable time. Dowie in his prime, soaring to new heights in the Spirit of God. Yet, even amid such blessing, the old Dowie didn't quite take a backseat. There is no doubt he did enjoy a good fight! But it was one of the less savoury aspects of his personality and tainted his ministry.

Disputes over planning permission for the church building led to a fine from the local Fitzroy Council,[19] followed by more arguments with the Council about the legality of street processions.[20] This ran into yet more disputes with the church landowner about the terms of the lease.[21] The landlord claimed the church unilaterally decided to change the payment terms. He called foul and locked the congregation out until they paid the full agreed price.

As a result, Dowie's street processions were less by choice and more by necessity. He kept advertising services, and thousands of people turned up in Johnstone Street to a locked building. What could he do Dowie thought to himself but have a street procession? It was his legal right and his Christian duty.[22]

The Fitzroy Police were understandably less than enthusiastic. They were concerned about public order and arrested him to put a stop to the processions.

They didn't reckon on the drawing power of a good story. The more times Dowie turned up in court, the more stories the press run, and the more people came to his church to see what was going on and ended up in the impromptu street processions.[23]

Dowie immensely enjoyed his moment in the public eye and relished the prospect of being "imprisoned for the gospel," making great capital of it. At his court appearance he argued with dramatic flourish, he must obey the law of God, rather than that of man. If the court wanted its pound of flesh, he had fourteen stone to choose from, but no money as he had given it all away rather than pay a fine![24]

The Magistrates made clear they would rather he just went away and stopped bothering them than give over a pound of his ample flesh. But they were in a quandary as Dowie resolutely refused to pay any fines imposed. Eventually, they lost patience and imprisoned him for thirty days.[25]

With the first sentence served, Dowie turned up for another court appearance, this time with five others from his church. The court sentenced him to a further seven days imprisonment.

Dowie's congregation were outraged and made complaints to the Solicitor General that the sentence passed was unduly harsh. The men locked up with Dowie had already given the court their word they would not take part in any more street processions.[26]

Fortunately, the Solicitor General saw sense and made a recommendation for their release, after receiving Dowie's pledge to stop holding processions.[27]

In the absence of a church building and with street processions off-limits, Dowie's church met in the local town hall until they raised enough money to pay off their landlord.[28] Finally, in July 1885, they went back into their building in Johnstone Street.

It was all over, bar the inevitable arms and legs the story grew in Dowie's telling and re-telling of his imprisonment for the gospel by the 'ungodly' Magistrates of Fitzroy.[29]

EXPLOSION

The high profile strategy made the headlines and filled the Tabernacle with the curious, but it also proved dangerous.

Dowie had many enemies. Some of them opposed his temperance beliefs; others just wanted to cause trouble. Whatever their motives, he was now very much in the public eye and that made him incredibly vulnerable.

He found out just how much so only a few months later in September 1885.

It was well into the evening, and four baptismal candidates stood outside Dowie's church office waiting to speak with him.

But sitting at his desk, Dowie could find no peace. All day long, he sensed something was wrong.[30] A life insurance policy, filled in earlier that day, kept coming back to torment him.[31]

Suddenly an audible voice pierced the air, "Rise. Go!"

Quickly clearing his papers from the desk, Dowie told his assistant to get everyone out of the building. He would be back first thing tomorrow and would see them all then.

Dowie's Tabernacle.

ATTEMPT TO BLOW IT UP.

Evening News, 4 Sept 1885

After a restless night, Dowie arrived at the church to find his office demolished by a dynamite explosion, set directly under his desk! The floorboards lay scattered haphazardly across the room, with debris everywhere.

The explosion would almost certainly have killed him if he had stayed any longer the night before.[32] Deeply shaken by the turn of events, Dowie realised it was an assassination attempt.

The Devil would try to kill by "outright violence, if not by disease."[33] He was a marked man. Satan had lost on this occasion, but he would be back.

TRAGEDY STRIKES

Two months later, Jeanie and Dowie were out of town on a healing mission. They returned to find their three children all ill. Though Gladstone and Esther were recovering, six-year-old Jeanie remained weak and listless.[34]

'Jeanie *secondus*' was her daddy's angel. Sweet, fragile and adoring. His treasure. He survived the lonely nights in temporary lodgings in the dark days, thinking of going home to his angel and her big, wet kisses covering his face.[35]

Now his baby was sick. His baby was dying. For most of the day, Dowie sat with little Jeanie in his lap, hugging her close, desperately hoping her fragile frame would absorb some life from him. Something happened to Dowie that day that caused his faith to fail when he needed it most. Jeanie went downhill fast. She took a fit. When Dowie prayed over her, he seemed to hear a voice say, "The fit will cease, and the Lord will take her."[36]

He told his wife of the words, and they both agreed to let their child go. A doctor was called to give a medical prognosis and so avoid an autopsy. The doctor said there was no hope and within hours, Jeanie was dead.[37]

On the morning of his daughter's death, Dowie preached with tears running down his face, "But now she is dead, wherefore should I fast? Can I bring her back again? I shall go to her, but she shall not return to me."[38]

Dowie carried the scars of Jeanie's death to his grave. In later years, his attitude hardened. He came to believe the voice was not from God but rather demonic.[39] And even years later, neither he nor his wife could put into words what happened to little Jeanie that night. It became, "an unwritten and unspoken chapter" in their lives.[40]

But even as he buried his beloved angel, Dowie resolved to go on believing in the "saving, healing and sanctifying power and love through faith in Jesus Christ, our Lord."[41]

THE FELLOWSHIP OF THE SPIRIT

God was gracious to Dowie and Jeanie. In the midst of their sorrow, yet more waves of the Holy Spirit deluged their lives.

Jeanie longed to pray for others for healing, but she was afraid to step out in faith. One evening in the Tabernacle, a group stayed behind and began to bring their deepest desires to God in prayer. Jeanie asked the Lord to take away her fearful heart and give her the power to speak. God heard Jeanie's cry and gave her what she called, "a gracious answer" -

> Immediately I felt the strengthening power of the Holy Spirit go through me, the chair against which I knelt shook, my backbone was strengthened and through and through me, I felt thrills of Divine power. I do not know how else to describe it but that it was a physical manifestation of spiritual power.[42]

Jeanie began to pray for people at the Johnstone Street Tabernacle and later accompanied her husband on a mission trip to Ballarat. As they travelled, he stopped to buy a newspaper and casually pointed out an advertisement he had placed in the local newspaper.

Jeanie almost fell off her chair when she saw her name listed as the speaker that night! "Oh, John, how could you?" she asked aghast.

He was unfazed and replied, "I thought you asked God to give you the power to speak for him; do you not believe that you were answered?"[43] As far as he was concerned, that settled it! Jeanie overcame her fears and gave an inspiring message on divine healing that evening and from then on, ministered alongside Dowie.

POWER FROM ON HIGH

Dowie had told Boardman three years before he left for world mission - and three years it was. Three years packed full of teaching on divine healing that laid a firm foundation for his later ministry.

The letter to Boardman he agonised so much over was added as an appendix to the report of the 1885 Conference. It was one of the most important events of the new divine healing movement and reports made their way across the world. Letters began to pour into Dowie's office from Europe, New Zealand and Australia with invitations to minister.[44]

In 1886, he spent six months on a mission in New Zealand setting up his new *Divine Healing Associations*.[45] He told Jeanie of his surprise when he moved in the gift of revelation and was able "to penetrate the deepest thoughts" of four different men.[46] And yet another vision of the "lights" they first saw in 1884.[47]

God was taking him to a new revelation of who he was in Christ,

> It is a fresh baptism of "Power from on High" and I am sure it is given me for witness and for service. I am so firm, cool, calm but so changed in feeling. Wave after wave of Holy Power has come upon me, and it remains. All else seems trivial compared to this.[48]

Something new and wonderful was happening. They were "being thrust out as well as led out." What a work that God would have for them if only they would be faithful to their calling![49]

SEVENTY TESTIMONIES

At the close of 1887, the *Divine Healing Association Fifth Annual Commemoration Services* celebrated five years of Dowie's ministry and five years of God's goodness. Seventy testimonies of divine healing were given, many in person, others by letter.

John Dillon Thomas

Stories like that of young John Dillon Thomas, whose arm was saved from amputation through Dowie's prayers.[50] Mary Philbin who testified her daughter received healing from swollen limbs and another daughter of neuralgia.[51] Mrs Moon who said four years before she had a tumour on her liver and her doctor said surgery was the only hope. But she was healed after Dowie's prayers with no further recurrence.[52] Miss Trickett testified to instant healing from liver and kidney problems. She called herself - "A living wonder, raised up to tell others what the Lord can and will and is waiting to do."[53]

Mrs Lacey said she attended a Dowie meeting but was unable to see Dowie in person. She later asked a friend to request prayer and, at the moment Dowie prayed, she received instant healing.[54] Mrs Colley's daughter received healing from measles within three hours of Dowie's prayers. The little girl was only five years old and "of great faith."[55]

Dowie signed off his report of the Conference by summing up his ministry as a Free Christian Minister. He had exercised his ministry "amidst many strange and stirring scenes." He loved them, but it was time to move on in obedience to God's call.[56]

In January 1888, Elders Joseph Grierson and John S. Wallington were ordained to lead the Free Christian Church in Fitzroy. In turn, they presented Dowie with a hundred pounds as a small token of thanks for his "untiring and devoted zeal in bringing very many in these lands from darkness into God's marvellous light and for the promotion of Divine Healing."[57]

On 3 March 1888, Dowie, Jeanie and their children Gladstone and Esther boarded the *Maranoa*, with hundreds of well-wishers gathered to see them off. After two months in New Zealand, ministering in the Divine Healing Associations,[58] they set sail for America.

7 AMERICAN FIRSTFRUITS

Dowie and Jeanie

*"I worked harder than all of them, yet not I but the grace
of God that was with me."*
1 Corinthians 15:10

ON 7 JUNE 1888 Dowie and Jeanie arrived at the Golden Gate,
San Francisco with two excited children and a combined total of
seventy-five dollars in their pockets.

As he looked out over San Francisco, a thrill of anticipation
ran through him. This was only the first leg of their world tour.
What did God have in store for them in this new country?

Dowie wasn't averse to giving God a helping hand, and before arrival placed a series of advertisements in the local press. Now he couldn't wait to get started.

HEALING THROUGH FAITH IN JESUS

The Rev. John Alex. Dowie and Mrs. Dowie,

OF MELBOURNE, VICTORIA, ARE EX-pected to arrive from Australia per P. M. S. S. Alameda, on or about the 15th of May, and they intend (D. V.) to conduct a Mission in this city en route to the Eastern States and Europe. Friends desiring to communicate will please address their letters care of Messrs. J. D. SPRECKELS & BROS., 327 Market street, San Francisco.

Daily Alta, 28 April 1888

But disappointingly, the first week in America proved little more than a series of shallow encounters with Christian Scientists, who thronged to meet him at the Palace Hotel.[1] Never known for his patience in long-suffering, Dowie quickly wearied of it all. Was there no end to their empty talk? He didn't come all the way to America for this!

FIRST MIRACLE OF THE MISSION

On 16 June at mid-afternoon, tired and hungry, he asked them all to leave for the day. As he turned to walk away, an old woman with eyes "like a spirit looking out of a house of suffering," arrested his attention.[2]

Lunch forgotten, Dowie stopped to speak with her. Elizabeth Browne told him she was from Sacramento. That morning, she made the painful journey to the Palace Hotel, hobbling with her crutch. The doctors said she needed an operation, but Mrs Browne was afraid of operations. Three different doctors diagnosed part of her anklebone needed to come off.

The old lady was afraid she would lose her whole foot and said she would rather die with it "in that fix" than have an operation.[3] She told Dowie the strange events that brought her to the hotel that morning. Though her family weren't religious, on the previous day her husband read an interview with Dowie in the local newspaper. He had no time for preachers which made it even more surprising when he said,

> That is the old-time religion. Or else it is all a lie, go down and see if the doctor is what they say he is and if he is, you will come back cured.[4]

So here she was, come to see if the "old time religion" could do anything for her. Just enough faith to get that far - not enough courage to open her mouth in amongst a crowd of strangers. For six hours, Elizabeth sat quietly at the Palace Hotel, watching it all happen around her, crutch by her side.[5]

Suddenly, there was the Doctor asking if she was a Christian! Why she didn't know, she replied in surprise. How could she know something like that? She couldn't even read.

Dowie smiled at her simplicity. What a refreshing change from those "fine-feathered birds with polluted hearts"[6] who twittered around him for days! After leading Elizabeth in a heartfelt prayer for salvation, Dowie sensed she was in a place where faith could rise. She was open to experiencing the supernatural, not just talking about it.[7]

He asked, "If Jesus were to enter this room now and to present himself to you, would you ask him to heal you, believing that he would?"

"Yes," she answered.

"Then he is here."

She looked puzzled.

"Invisibly present," Dowie told her. "He is always invisibly present."[8]

Elizabeth understood. The best-educated preachers of Dowie's day failed to understand what Elizabeth Browne understood. Jesus was present to heal. Dowie took her diseased foot in his hands and spoke out a prayer of faith. The power of God immediately fell upon the old woman, and the pain left her foot!

She was in shock, crying out, "Doctor I am healed, I am healed!"

It was a beautiful moment when God reached out and embraced a tired old woman the world had labelled nothing but "poor white trash."[9] Laughter mingled with tears, as she reached out and hugged her daughter for the first time in years.

After thanking Dowie profusely, Elizabeth stood to walk away. She had only taken a few steps when he called after her, "You've left something belonging to you."

"What?" she called back.

"Your crutch."

"Keep it," she cried jubilantly. "I don't need it!"[10]

It was the first miracle of the mission and the first trophy seized from the enemy. An old rugged and redundant wooden crutch. Many more would follow. Four months later Elizabeth testified,

> He told me to get up and walk, and I walked right off, and I can walk now, and I am pretty old - not so very pretty but old…From that day to this I have never felt any pain like that I had before, nor any pain in that foot and it is quite well, it is very well.[11]

After Elizabeth had spoken, Dowie added,

> We have heard talk about Divine healings not standing; there is the first. If they do not stand it is not because there is any failure in God's work of healing, the failure is in the person healed. Let our aged sister's story be a lesson to some who think themselves to be something when they are nothing. She had no opinion of herself, and therefore, the Lord healed, and the Lord keeps her.[12]

Elizabeth Browne may have been poorly educated, but she certainly wasn't stupid. She didn't need a college degree to understand pain. She hobbled in with a crutch and walked out without one. And one Mrs Browne testifying was better than a hundred healing sermons. People were tired of words – they wanted to see the power of God at work. And they saw it when Dowie came to town.

AMERICAN FIRSTFRUITS

Over the weeks to follow, Dowie held services at the local YMCA and preached in churches that were open to him. In a typical meeting, 'God's Witnesses to Divine Healing' stepped forward to tell of the most extraordinary miracles.

Delilah King

In August 1888 seventy-one-year-old Delilah King testified to the healing of throat cancer after doctors treated her unsuccessfully for four years. When she went to Dowie for prayer, the cancer had already destroyed one tonsil and part of her tongue. But at Oakland Presbyterian Church, God gloriously healed her.[13]

Georgie Ritchville, blind from birth, testified he could now see.[14] Mrs Coffin, suffering from the age of three with ulcerated legs, arrived in Dowie's meeting with crutches and now could walk after twenty-six years a cripple.[15]

Miss Amy F. Wilcox received salvation and healing all at once. Dowie told his audience that he didn't lay a finger on Miss Wilcox, just prayed, "I never touched her; she laid down her crutches, and she walked back to her seat without them, and she has been walking ever since."[16]

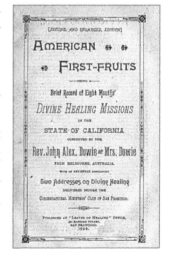

These were extraordinary miracles and led to more and more sufferers seeking Dowie out for prayer. He lived at a pace few could_match and his days were a whirlwind of activity. The publication of *American Firstfruits* in 1889 took the stories of

'God's Witnesses' out to a wider audience, and after only a year in America, six Divine Healing Associations were in operation, with a combined membership of seventeen hundred.

A quarter of a million tracts were distributed and ten thousand of Dowie's pamphlets sold. A thousand people had professed salvation, and ten thousand accepted the doctrine of divine healing.[17] Not bad for an initial missionary budget of seventy-five dollars!

NO CESSATION

Dowie's theology of healing was virtually identical to the early days in Australia. Jesus was good, and the Devil was bad. However added to that, he now confidently taught on the gifts of the Holy Spirit. Addressing a group of Congregational ministers, he told them,

> We teach what is recorded in the 12th chapter of First Corinthians, that "the gifts of healings" are in the Holy Spirit, like all the other gifts of God. They are not under the control of a body called the Church; they are not controlled by any person, call them by what office or title you may. They are in the Holy Spirit, and if the Holy Spirit be in you, he will divide to severally as he wills.[18]

According to Dowie in the absence of the gifts functioning, a pernicious lie had crept into the church that God 'wills' disease. Embalmed in songs and taught from pulpits, he was determined to root out that lie, wherever he found it.[19]

He wearied of the pious biographies that spoke of people

glorifying God in their illness. They would have glorified God more in a healthy body and able to work for him![20] Ministers, who preached sickness to be the will of God, should thank God when they got ill because that would make them holy. Instead, they went running off to doctors to try and get better!

THE HONEYMOON IS OVER

His message was a radical challenge to leaders in the established church. If it were true, what did it mean for their ministries? What did it mean for their positions in society? For many, the shutters went down. The man was a zealot and a firebrand. They had seen his like before, and he would soon fizzle out.

Although he wanted a ministry that was "irrespective of all sects or parties,[21] theological America gave Dowie the cold shoulder. He was "assailed with incredible bitterness by some of our fellow-shepherds."[22] A representative of the Los Angeles Divine Healing Society told the *Los Angeles Herald* that Dowie was a preacher of "exceptional enthusiasm and power" but, "the religious people of the city are very far, however, from being of one on the subject of the teachings of Mr Dowie."[23]

An article from the *Oakland Inquirer* gives an insight into that animosity. It was written by the Reverend E. C. Chapman at the request of the Oakland Pastors' Union. Dowie scathingly dismissed it as, "a manifesto of the whole Pastors' Union against divine healing."[24] He responded to their criticisms at the First Baptist Church, Oakland on 27 January 1889 asking,

> Why do our critics not venture, if our doctrine is "unscriptural and false" to give us a single passage of Scripture to prove it so?[25]

Much of what the Oakland pastors put up against Dowie was the old story of "better not to have faith than to have it, as you might be disappointed." A bare-bones misery theology of "God made me sick, to make me holy." But they also attacked Dowie's belief that divine healing must always come; it is the "full privilege" of the believer to walk in divine health; and that any unanswered prayer must be the result of sin. The Oakland ministers claimed this was patently untrue.

That was an important and fundamental challenge to Dowie's doctrine. Dealing honestly and openly with it could arguably have strengthened his position. On the other hand, pioneers have to fight their corner, and that can push them to a place where they are unwilling to give an inch, for fear of losing a mile.

When accused by these ministers of being a fanatic, Dowie spoke of the time he visited John Knox's grave,

> ...it was the fanaticism of John Knox which brought Scotland to the feet of Christ. As I stood over that grave, I thanked God for John Knox. He was a so-called "fanatic." I hope you will all be such "fanatics." A man who knows nothing about this work calls it fanaticism and his ignorance is his excuse. A man who only cares for dollars and dimes will call it fanaticism, for it is a gratuitous ministry and he measures all things by his standard.[26]

His words did not go down well. Three days later, the Oakland First Baptist Church unanimously voted to exclude Dowie from using their building - one of the last open to him in the district.[27]

DOWIE MOVES ON

He moved further afield, ministering on the Pacific Coast from San Diego to Victoria, British Columbia and founding Divine Healing Associations as he went.[28] When churches closed their doors, he rented halls to speak in. It was all one to him. God had not called him to build a reputation but a Kingdom.

Yet Dowie's blind spot to other peoples' views and in particular, the validity of other divine healing ministries, worked against him. In 1890, he invited A.B. Simpson on a mission tour of divine healing. Referring to his Four-Fold Gospel, Simpson replied, "No, Brother Dowie, I have four wheels on my chariot. I cannot agree to neglect the other three while I devote all my time to the one."[29]

Simpson's rebuttal led to a rift between the two men, with Dowie later calling into question the miracles that took place under Simpson.[30] Dowie also rejected Maria Woodworth-Etter's ministry as "trance evangelism" and occultic.[31] The *Oakland Tribune* gleefully reported,

> "Satan," said Brother Dowie, with special reference to Sister Woodworth, "deceives women today as much as he did Eve in the Garden of Eden."[32]

For Dowie, there was only one way of doing things – his way. As Simpson's associate Dr Kenneth MacKenzie wryly summed up, "Born rulers wisely seek and receive counsel from those who may be competent to advise them. Dr Dowie had no peers. Aids in his work he counted by the score. But they were followers only."[33]

JENNIE'S HEALING

Despite, or maybe because of, Dowie's rugged individualism, Jennie Paddock's healing set him on a course that propelled him to a worldwide ministry in divine healing.

Jennie Paddock

The occasion was the *Chicago International Divine Healing Association Conference* in August 1890 at Western Springs, a suburb of Chicago. Dowie was about to launch into an attack on Simpson's Christian Alliance, when a woman stepped forward with a prayer request for a Mrs Jennie Paddock, suffering from a large fibroid tumour.[34]

When Dowie received the prayer request, Jennie was some fifteen miles away in a semi-comatose state and hours away from death. Her family had gathered around her bed, waiting for the inevitable.

The miracle was one of simple faith. When he prayed, her sleep became sound and natural. On the next morning, Jennie's eyes opened wide, and she shouted out praise and glory to God. Instantaneously, she knew Jesus had healed her! Dowie took the miracle as a sign from Heaven that his theology of healing was correct. He decided to remain in Chicago and moved his base to Evanston in October 1890.[35]

Chicago's newspapers were unimpressed with the city's new arrival, with the *Chicago Tribune* dismissing him as, "an apostle of the 'faith cure' - a mode of treatment which caused the confinement of some of its professors in penal establishments and other in insane asylums."[36]

Dowie was determined to prove them all wrong. His sights were set on the upcoming Chicago Fair when he knew the eyes of the world would be on the city. Where better to showcase his gospel of divine healing?

8 THE LITTLE WOODEN HUT

"The people were amazed when they saw the mute speaking, the crippled made well, the lame walking and the blind seeing..."

Matthew 15:31

THE CHICAGO FAIR CELEBRATED the "glories and mysteries of human achievement"[1] ironically at a time when the brave new world confronted the same poverty and inequality that blighted the tired old one.

Crippling national recession gripped America, with unemployment and homelessness rife. Closer to home, Chicago government officials were corrupt, rubbish piled up on the streets, and impoverished immigrants struggled to survive in the land of reputed opportunity.[2]

But on a positive note, the Fair brought jobs for the workers, visitors with money to spend and a welcome escape from reality for everyone else. It lifted the heads of the downtrodden Chicago citizens, with the very best of innovation and invention on show and cultural input from worlds old and new.[3]

For a season, it seemed as though the world had come to see Chicago in all its glory, as the Queen of Sheba once went to Solomon to gaze upon his splendour.

The paying public generally like a little bit of whooping and hollering with their culture to make sure they get their money's worth. So no surprise then that Buffalo Bill Cody's Wild West Show on East 62nd Street proved a major attraction with crowds of up to eighteen thousand people gathered daily to "Oooh" and "Ahhh" at the blood-curdling scenes.

Opposite the Wild West Show stood a shabbily-constructed building, proudly flying the flag - *Christ is All*. Few noticed it. There was far too much else to see. But amongst "the glories and mysteries of human achievement," God had set up his own show, in a Little Wooden Hut.

THE LITTLE WOODEN HUT

Dowie built Zion Tabernacle with his own hands, assisted by the Chicago Branch of the International Divine Healing Association. The land cost a sizable $10,000 and the building itself only $2,000 to construct.[4]

It showed. In truth, it wasn't much more than a big shed. But the sign outside belied its humble appearance,

> *Zion Tabernacle, Headquarters of the International Divine Healing Association, Rev John Alex Dowie, Founder and President. 'Christ Is All and in All.'*

The Tabernacle opened on 7 May 1893, the first Sunday following the launch of the Fair. After an inauspicious beginning, unfortunately, it didn't get much better. Numbers topped about fifty, with most of the chairs sitting forlorn and empty, while a handful of people gathered at the front listening to Dowie preach.

Chicago was much too occupied, as Dowie put it, with drinking, "the Polluted Cup of her Vanity Fair and dreaming away the voluptuous hours."[5]

(Well that and Buffalo Bill).

Every party must come to an end, and with "the polluted cup" drained dry, the Fair closed in October 1893. Everyone packed up and went home, leaving the sad remnants of the "glories and mysteries of human achievements" to offer refuge to the homeless in the long, cold winter months to follow.

Dowie stayed put. Although numbers had picked up at the Tabernacle, the freezing temperatures saw attendance plummet. The Little Wooden Hut bravely stood its ground, in true pioneer spirit, boldly proclaiming the Lordship of Christ over Chicago. Mocked, despised but mostly ignored.

Dowie was no stranger to toughing it out. He was on a

mission to bring divine healing to Chicago and stayed his course, praying that God would give him a breakthrough. Money was so tight; there was little left over to pay the rent in his nearby rented accommodation. And now he had the debt from the Tabernacle against his name.[6] There were no regrets, Dowie told himself as he walked down East 62nd Street, his collar turned up against the cold. God would surely come.

GOD IS IN THE HOUSE

God did come. By the spring of 1894, miracles of healing broke out, leading to "thousands upon thousands" flocking to the Little Wooden Hut.[7]

The Tabernacle buzzed with excitement. In every corner, stories of healing and salvation were elatedly told and retold, with every chair taken and every spot filled.

Wave after wave of divine power swept over the people,

resulting in multiple conversions and divine healings. Lucy Gaston, the editor of the *Harvey Citizen*, attended and said she had to pinch herself, "to find out if I really was in the nineteenth century or whether I was in the time of Christ."[8]

The inside of the Tabernacle was breath-taking - its walls adorned with stars, crowns and crosses made of trophies captured from the enemy - crutches, boots, trusses, braces, Masonic paraphernalia, medicine bottles and rosaries. Even some burglar tools and revolvers! Two letters stood out on the wall, formed of boxes of cigars - S and P. They stood for *Stink-Pot* - Dowie's favourite expression for smokers. He wasn't letting Abaddon off lightly!

As the fame of Zion Tabernacle spread, the Devil put in a personal appearance. A visiting minister ridiculed it as "a miserable wooden hut"[9], and a University of Chicago professor sneered it was nothing but "a little bit of kindling wood."[10]

The professor would have done well to remember God chose another little hut – a lowly stable – to bring his Son into the world. But Dowie got mileage out of the spiteful words and retaliated he would take his "little bit of kindling wood" and use it to set the world on fire![11]

A SCENE FROM THE GOSPELS

It was no empty boast. People congregated around Dowie, as they once went to Jesus in Galilee. He carried a greater anointing than anything seen in America, or indeed anywhere in the world, in the history of the modern church. He had a grace upon his life at that time that enabled him to keep going, praying for thousands each week and seeing multiple healing miracles.

Arthur Newcomb, later associate editor of *Leaves of Healing*, gave an account of a typical service from these early days –

All classes, the poor and the rich, were represented in the congregation numbering 2,000 that occupied the chairs, stood in the aisles, fringed the walls and standing outside, hoisted the windows and craned their necks, not to see but to hear. The gathering was a solemn one and so piteous. Long before the hour set for the services to begin, the Tabernacle was crowded.

Arthur Newcomb

Carriages drove up to the door, and stricken people were lifted from them and carried in. Mothers brought misshapen children in their arms and went in. The feeble, with tottering steps, were helped in by friends. The bed-ridden were born in on stretchers. The sightless were there.

The deaf had fingered out to them the hope held out. The thump of crutches was heard, as hundreds thus enabled to walk, came in. It was a piteous spectacle, the sight of these afflicted ones - men, women and children. A host of men came, blind, deaf, or paralysed. Women came, worn, suffering and painmarked. Young girls, fresh-faced but marred in body. Children, bright-eyed, intelligent, well grown but helpless. How intently, too, did all listen, how eager and expectant and hope betrayed its presence in the face of even him whose case, in a physical sense, was the least hopeful. They prayed fervently—they wept, many a man, many a

*woman, many a child in that oddly assorted gathering, whether
there as a supplicant or as sturdy, healthful helpmate or friend of
the afflicted, wept.*[12]

For the hopeless, suddenly there was hope in Zion Tabernacle.
God had come to visit his people with healing power once more.

LET THE LITTLE CHILDREN COME

Thursday was Children's Day and given over entirely to praying
with children and their mothers. Dowie adapted the message of
divine healing so that even the youngest could understand, with
designated rooms set aside for those too ill to take part in the
bigger groups. Newcomb wrote,

> *He frequently calls upon many whose little legs have
> been lengthened, deaf and dumb who can now speak
> and hear, some who have never walked from their
> birth who can now walk and leap and run and all sorts
> of children to testify to their healing.*
>
> *Their mothers stand up with them and tell the simple
> story. On that day, there are children everywhere, and
> often Dr Dowie lays hands upon over five hundred
> children, seeing them in the prayer-room in well-
> ordered and quiet companies of eighty to one hundred.
> As many as twenty different nationalities are
> sometimes represented on Children's day.*[13]

There are multiple testimonies of children healed under
Dowie's ministry. Stories like that of Billy Esser, born with one
leg shorter than the other. After prayer, he could "walk up and
down the floor, without crutch or brace or boot."[14]

Billy Esser

Ten-year-old Katie Keck was due to have her leg amputated. After prayer, she could run the length of the Tabernacle without any pain. Dowie rejoiced and asked, "Mr Theological Professor, what are you going to make of her? She ought now, according to the dictates of medical and surgical "science" to be lying in Mercy Hospital with a bleeding stump and a broken heart."[15]

What indeed? These miracles defied explanation and God's 'show' drew visitors from all around the world.

Katie Keck

Yet, even with such powerful testimonies, the voice of the Pharisee still rang out. One critic accepted the services were full but argued these people were mostly, "from abroad." He went on, "the great majority of Chicago people have become disgusted with the whole thing."[16]

That may have been true in some quarters. However, William Stead in his study of Chicago in 1894, lambasted the respectable religious people of Chicago for breathing new life into "the grim old Calvinistic doctrine of reprobation," to justify walking away from those in need in their city.

After all, if God didn't care about them, why should they?[17] Their God was no friend to the poor.

Was there ever a more damning indictment of the apostate church? And was there ever a more decisive repudiation given by God than in the Little Wooden Hut? In Zion Tabernacle, from the least to the greatest, they were all made welcome by the 'non-respectable' Holy Spirit.

CENTRAL MUSIC HALL

Soon the huge numbers in attendance proved too much for the Little Wooden Hut, and Dowie rented the Chicago Central Music Hall for his Sunday gatherings. The *Chicago Inter Ocean* reported on the first service on 15 April 1894,

> Central Music Hall was packed from floor to ceiling yesterday afternoon with persons drawn either by necessity, sympathy or curiosity to hear the Rev John Alexander Dowie and the testimonies of those who had been cured of their diseases through his ministry. If the hall had been twice its size, it could have been filled easily by the crowds that were turned away.[18]

Other newspapers gave less positive accounts but nevertheless related that divine healings were taking place.[19] Some saw Dowie as a fanatic but not a real threat to the status quo. That would change when he began to encroach into the domain of medicine. At that time, addictive morphine-based medicines were freely available at pharmacies and liberally used for a variety of ailments. According to Dowie, "devotion to their diabolical drugs" was the "principal disease" he saw when praying for people.[20] He needed to break that link to see people set free.

Amanda Hicks, Principal of Clinton Academy, was a case in point. In January 1894, she travelled an excruciating four hundred miles, lying on a makeshift cot, to see Dowie after years of debilitating illness.[21]

He immediately demanded she gave up her addictive drugs. After "a hand to hand struggle," she was set free from morphine addiction and healed. Amanda's local newspaper the *Clinton Democrat* published her story that she came home with "her eye as bright and her carriage as erect as ever in the days before her illness."[22]

Amanda Hicks

The publicity that came out of stories like Amanda's healing led to a massive increase in requests for places at Dowie's 'Healing Home.' More and more visitors poured in from out of town, and Dowie desperately needed extra space to keep up with demand.

HEALING HOMES

In May 1894 he bought a two-storey hotel at 6020 Egerton Avenue, to convert into Divine Healing Home No 1 and use as his family home. He then leased another building next door to Zion Tabernacle for an additional Healing Home, and then yet another, at 6034 Egerton Avenue.

People came to Healing Homes from across America and further afield. They met the immediate need for board and lodging for visitors, but more importantly, created an environment where faith could rise. Martha Wing Robinson, who later opened her own divine healing home, wrote to a friend from a Dowie Healing Home,

> The conversations here would astonish anyone who
> stepped into the Home and did not know what was
> going on. Groups gather together and talk about God
> and Christ just as if they were personal friends.[23]

Martha stayed for two months, before returning home to
Davenport, totally healed.[24] Sadie Cody, the niece of Buffalo Bill,
was another notable visitor. An accident at the Chicago Fair
rendered Sadie a helpless cripple, with her flesh rotting over a
crumbling spine. She weighed eighty-five pounds and was
unable to support her weight. When she arrived at the Healing
Home her uncle, a medical doctor, took the address for her
funeral arrangements.

After five weeks in the Home, Sadie went back to her family,
totally healed. Dowie joked, "He (Buffalo Bill) captured Indians.
We have captured a Cody from the murderous demons of
disease!"[25] Fifteen years on, Sadie gave her testimony again at
Stone Church, Chicago. Her paralysis never returned, she was
now baptised in the Holy Spirit, speaking in tongues and about to
start a new job as secretary to divine healer Carrie Judd
Montgomery.[26]

THE LITTLE WHITE DOVE

No matter how many people Dowie prayed for and preached to,
it was never enough. He wanted to reach the world with his
gospel of divine healing. Out of that longing, came a worldwide
publishing ministry which prepared the way for the coming of
the early Pentecostal movement. He first trialled his signature
magazine *Leaves of Healing* in 1888 in Christchurch, New

Zealand, and then in San Francisco, but a lack of funds held him back.[27]

By 1894, he was ready to go again and set up Zion Publishing House with second-hand printing equipment.

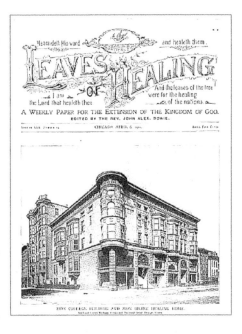

The first issue of the relaunched *Leaves of Healing* rolled off the press in August 1894 with Dowie's Covenanter symbol the 'Little White Dove' taking pride of place at the head of every copy.

The magazine was a phenomenal success in taking the doctrine of divine healing to millions worldwide, and by 1898 an estimated three-quarters of a million copies of *Leaves of Healing* circulated annually.[28]

Translations in German, French, Danish, Norwegian, Dutch, Chinese and Japanese went out from Zion post room to the corners of the globe. It became the 'Bible' of Dowie's movement, both at home and abroad. If people couldn't come to Zion - Zion would come to them because, as Dowie put it, "Wherever the Holy Dove goes, there the seed is dropped."[29]

Divine healing testimonies formed the heart of *Leaves of Healing* message. Dowie boasted these were "not the testimonies of "Mr Nobody who lives Nowhere…You look along the *Leaves of Healing*, and you will find the names and addresses of the people healed. The people can be found. They stand as living witnesses."[30]

DOWIE USING THE PRAYING-MACHINE.

Dowie's vision was for the world, and he wanted the world to know it. He prayed every morning at nine, using a time stamp for prayer requests, and called all of Zion to pray with him.

Jennie Lake, the wife of evangelist John Lake, recovered from a debilitating illness, after one of Dowie's regular nine o'clock morning prayer sessions.[31] Her husband and family set up a Dowie outreach in Sault Ste. Marie in Michigan.

Mr and Mrs George L. Flower, parents of J. Roswell Flower, attended a Dowie outreach in Toronto, Canada. Mrs Flower testified to the healing of her neighbour John Easton. Easton was forced to wear a plaster cast for six years, as his spine could not support him.[32] After prayer, he was totally restored.

Others healed at this time include early Pentecostals F.A. Graves, cured of epilepsy[33] and Lilian Yeoman, delivered from morphine addiction.[34]

Seven-year-old Cora Carley was healed after three years of deafness.[35] William Dinius, pastor of the Dowie outreach in Harvey, healed of sunstroke.[36] John Lake's younger brother Fred healed of kidney disease and his sister Maggie of breast cancer.[37]

Mary Dowling, healed of blindness.[38] Ida Lowrie of cancer.[39] Albion Wyman of consumption.[40] Linda Karch of deafness.[41] May Lohman of lameness.[42] R.F. Palm of facial cancer.[43] Charles Davis and Alma Keller, both healed of lameness. [44]

In the church services, in the Healing Homes, in the outreaches springing up across the world, there are scores of testimonies to healing miracles through Dowie's prayers. His star was on the rise, and it seemed that he was unstoppable.

9 YEAR OF PERSECUTION

Divine Healing Home 1

"Pink pills for pale people and pale pills for pink people."
John Alexander Dowie

CHICAGO HAD NEVER SEEN anything like it. Far from being a passing fad, Dowie was invading the city with Heaven. Shock and incredulity gave way to howls of indignant outrage as newspaper columnists railed at this so-called charlatan.

Advertising unregulated 'medicinal cures' and addictive opiates was routine business for them – but these self-appointed guardians of public morality, the 'respectable' commercial press, were affronted at the claim that God can heal today. [1] They blasted the Healing Homes as a public health hazard, filled with the insane and infectious disease.[2] According to the *Chicago Tribune*, Dowie extracted money from sufferers with his bogus claims.[3] He shipped out bodies in the dead of night from "Dowie's Den."[4] His preaching drove people insane, to the point they needed to be incarcerated.[5]

When Dowie responded that the editor would get "a fight," if he didn't stop publishing slander, the *Tribune* hysterically reported, *"John Alexander Dowie Seeks Gore."*[6]

DIES IN DOWIE'S DEN

Body of an Unknown Inmate Is Removed at Night.

TAKEN TO THE MORGUE.

Police Learn It Is to Be Shipped Away This Morning.

THEY NOTIFY THE CORONER.

Investigation of the Mysterious Case Will Be Made.

Chicago Tribune, 2 July 1895

They dramatically told their readers Mayor Hopkins had designated three shifts of a hundred police officers to guard its offices day and night. The Fire Brigade assisted with the loan of a bright red extension ladder for staff to escape down, should Dowie breach the police defences and come up to thrash the editor, Joseph Medill.

THE BOARD OF MEDICINE

Disappointingly for the *Tribune*, the expected offensive from the five-foot-four-inch Dowie and his crutch-wielding flock did not materialise, thus depriving them of yet another sensationalist headline.

But their campaign against Dowie received a new impetus from the Illinois Board of Medicine. An outbreak of smallpox at the World Fair had led to a thousand fatalities and brought the Board under pressure to justify their existence. The Board claimed the deaths were because people failed to be immunised.

Others argued it was because the Board was dysfunctional and corrupt.[7]

They needed to win back some respect in the eyes of the public and Dowie looked like an easy target. In June 1894, the *Tribune* printed an appeal from Board Secretary J.W. Scott for witnesses against Dowie,

> I am anxious to test the Illinois laws on Dowie and other faith healers and put a stop to their nonsense. If some of the people whom Dowie has practised upon will put themselves in communication with me, I will try our State law on him.[8]

They were determined to expose Dowie as a fraud and in January 1895 arrested him for 'unlawfully' practising medicine, with the *Tribune* confidently predicting, *"Dowie's Race is Nearly Run."*[9]

They didn't really think that one through. Dowie mocked,

> Now that is the richest joke I have ever heard. I, who am fighting medicine all the time, who for thirty years have never touched it and whose children have never tasted it since they were born - I am to be prosecuted for practising medicine without a licence! I fear they had been drinking champagne and got some real pain in their heads. The Lord have mercy upon them.[10]

When the case fell through the Board realised they needed a new strategy. A hastily drawn-up ordinance came out, expressly aimed at Dowie, that ruled all 'hospitals' required a permit and could not operate in residential areas without the consent of residents.

Divine Healing Home 3

Violation of the law would lead to a penalty of $50-100, with a hospital defined as "any place used for the reception or care, temporary or continuous of the sick, injured or dependent, including women awaiting confinement, or used for the treatment of mental or physical disease or body injury."[11]

This paved the way for the Board to assert all of the Dowie Healing Homes were illegal. They were confident this time they could shut him down for good.

DOWIE GOES TO WAR

Dowie came out fighting with his April 1895 article, *Doctors, Drugs and Devils, or the Foes of Christ the Healer.* All doctors were "poisoners-general and surgical butchers," "Molochs of Medicine," and "monsters who hold in their hands deadly poisons and deadly surgical knives."[12]

He could have been more measured. He wasn't; he was Dowie and criticism always brought out the worst in him. It was a self-limiting truth that Dowie had an inability to separate the foes of

Dowie, from the foes of Christ. Added to that, his theology of healing tended to leave him on the back foot. Dowie believed in every instance; the sufferer should get better. When that evidently didn't happen, as shown by the gruesome stories of bodies carted out from "Dowie's Den," he struggled to articulate an answer that made sense to the wider public.

Doctors, Drugs and Devils polarised an already deteriorating situation. In May 1895, the Commissioner of Health sent Dowie a form to register his Healing Homes as hospitals. Dowie wrote back to say the Homes were not hospitals. They were private residences, where people received prayer during their stay. He added,

> It is a pitiful sight to see the State Board of Health and the City Health Department moving against a good work at the insistence of a lying press and a concealed band of interested doctors who feel their craft is in danger because of tens of thousands of persons who are abandoning medicine and seeking and finding healing through faith in Jesus Christ.[13]

He did have a point. Stead claimed at that time Chicago had no ambulance service and untrained police officers collected the sick and injured from public places. A woefully inadequate six ambulances covered the entire city, two of which were reserved for sufferers of infectious illnesses. Many of the injured died on route to hospital or were left unattended at police stations. There were no hospice type facilities in Chicago or places to convalesce.[14]

The Board of Health supervised this shambolic state of affairs and their biggest concern was Dowie's Healing Homes, rather than reform their practices! But the Chicago press were not going to let the pitiful state of the city's public health care stand in the way of a good story. On 7 June 1895, the *Chicago Inter Ocean*, previously a supporter of Dowie under its former editor Herman H. Kohlsaat, added their weight to the moral outrage against the Healing Homes,

> Consumptives in the last stages are forced out into the most inclement weather to attend "divine" services, resulting in premature death. The violently insane, as well as the ordinary demented individuals, are harboured. None are denied admission provided they bring the necessary funds. Frequent deaths have occurred, and the bodies of the victims have been surreptitiously removed from the premises after nightfall.[15]

It was all getting a bit mean and nasty - but worse was to come when the Egerton Avenue residents banded together with their own version of neighbourhood watch.

THE FASHIONABLE PEOPLE

A week later, as Dowie was about to conduct an afternoon service, four men arrived with a warrant for his arrest on a charge of violation of the Hospital Ordinance. An undercover police officer had infiltrated Dowie's Healing Home.[16]

On the following day, they arrested him again on the same charge. This time one of his neighbours, George W. Riggs, had brought the charges. The neighbours protested Dowie's Homes devalued their properties, turning the Avenue into a place that was "bad and devilish."[17] Other residents hit back and said the sight of the sick was just too much of an uncomfortable reminder of the "real world" for the fashionable people of Egerton Avenue.[18]

The police dumped Dowie into the back of the 'wagon' and drove him around the streets, putting on a show for his neighbours. Corruption and bribery were rife at that time, and on their paltry wages, it was in their interests to stay on good terms with the fashionable people of the Avenue.

But, despite the explicit collusion between the police department, the neighbours and the Board of Health, the trying out of the Illinois laws on Dowie proved an expensive fiasco.

Although the Board argued the Homes were a health hazard,[19] Dowie robustly denied the charge, producing multiple witnesses to show infectious patients were kept isolated at all times.[20] When the lower courts convicted him, he appealed to the higher courts and kept his Homes open.[21]

His main line of defence was not about divine healing as such. Rather he argued, the hospital ordinance was far too broad in its scope. To follow it to the letter, no one could look after the sick. A mother caring for a sick baby would need a licence to practice medicine! This was clearly ludicrous and undue interference of the state in the lives of its citizens.

By the end of June, forty-six arrest warrants had been issued. On one occasion alone the neighbours, led by Leo J. Maguire, caused thirty-seven warrants to be issued for Dowie's arrest.[22]

Before the year was out, Dowie claimed a hundred arrest warrants in total were served on him.[23] He wearied of the whole thing and warned the press if they didn't leave him alone, he would sue and build "half a dozen Zions."[24]

SIX DAYS TO GET ARRESTED

ARRESTED IN HIS PULPIT.

Dowie, the Chicago Divine Healer, Again Placed In Jail.

Taken From Church by an Officer Amid the Protests of the Congregation.

San Francisco Call, 22 July 1895

On 21 July 1895, the Chicago authorities overstepped themselves, when the police arrested Dowie in the middle of a sermon. Chicago was not averse to persecuting faith healers but religious sentiments ran deep, and this seemed a step too far.

Even the *Tribune* expressed outrage at the action of the police. After filling multiple news columns with grisly stories about deaths in the Healing Homes, they now thought the authorities were "overdoing the Dowie business." It was unseemly to arrest him on a Sunday when "there are six secular days which can be devoted to arresting him."[25]

Dowie appealed to his old supporter, the influential Kohlsaat, now editor and proprietor of the *Times-Herald*. Kohlsaat, in turn, made representations to Mayor George Bell Swift. Up until then Swift had ignored Dowie's complaints about police harassment but relented on Kohlsaat's intervention.[26]

The tide was beginning to turn in Dowie's favour. His lawyers persuaded the court to dismiss forty-four cases against him and issue a temporary restraining order against the Board.

Although that was overturned, a second judge granted Dowie's petition to allow the jury to evaluate "the validity of the ordinance."[27]

The tables had turned with the ordinance itself now in the dock.[28] In December 1895, Cook County Superior Court ruled the hospital law invalid. They upheld the city's right to regulate hospitals but said the definition of a hospital was too broad.[29]

Dowie was jubilant. He took on bureaucracy, police and press and beat them all. What was more, throughout the year the people of Chicago opened up their newspapers to divine healing on trial.[30] It proved better than employing an army of publicists. Even the *Tribune* grudgingly admitted,

> The churches, police, health department all tried to suppress him and only proved themselves good advertising mediums. Dowie's following had become thousands instead of hundreds.[31]

No one could have done it, bar the indomitable Dowie. What on earth would he do next? Well, what would Jesus do if he came to Chicago?

10 THE
APOSTOLIC CHURCH

Dowie preaching

"If Christ came to Chicago...he would form a church..."
W.T. Stead

ON 22 JANUARY 1896, Dowie launched his new apostolic Christian Catholic Church in Zion.

He told the seven hundred people gathered at the opening event, the new body would replace the International Divine Healing Associations and all members could join, but must first leave their existing churches.

The Christian Catholic Church would do everything that Stead said Jesus' church in Chicago would do. Feed the hungry, minister to the prostitute and bring all of the Father's sheep into the one fold in the spirit of "catholicity."[1]

It was a 'catholic' church because it would encompass all.[2] And 'apostolic' because the office of an apostle was perpetual. But, Dowie told his hearers, he did not personally think he had reached "a deep enough depth of true humility" to accept such a calling.[3] For then, he was content to operate in the role of the General Overseer of the Christian Catholic Church.

Once the right structures were in place, God would honour them by fully restoring the nine-fold spiritual gifts and the apostolic and prophetic office.[4]

THE APOSTOLIC CHURCH

This type of exposition may have been new to Dowie's listeners but, as we alluded to earlier, it showed remarkable similarities to the beliefs of Edward Irving.

In 1832 one of Irving's followers wrote, "Mr Irving has been ejected from the Church of Scotland for daring to allow them (the gifts of the Spirit) a place and God will now clear a way for the reception of all his gifts, to gather and constitute an Apostolic church, to be set upon his holy hill of Zion.[5]

Dowie mirrored this when he said, "We, therefore, believe that that the Lord will "build up" in the little city of Zion, in the vicinity of Chicago and will rapidly extend throughout the world a Christian Catholic Apostolic Church."[6]

He saw himself as taking forward the divine commission given to Irving that was "stillborn" when Irving died, shortly after the formation of his own movement, the Catholic Apostolic Church.[7]

That divine commission was no less than the "restoration of the primitive church,"[8] and Dowie would ordain deaconesses, deacons, elders, pastors, teachers and preachers to "carry forward the work upon New Testament lines."[9]

Practically speaking, that was going to take money, and by consolidating all of his followers into one body, Dowie could maximise revenues to fund his dream of global expansion.[10] For when the Lord built up Zion, he would return in glory!

ZION GETS MOBILISED

Over the next few years, Zion saw extraordinary growth and success, and for a season, it seemed as though it might just happen.

The purchase of the Imperial Hotel at 1201 Michigan Avenue brought all of the Healing Homes into one building in Zion Home.

Zion Headquarters,
Michigan Avenue

Sunday services were held at the Chicago Auditorium from October 1895 to April 1896, with large crowds of between three to five thousand people filling the hall and an average of forty persons a week baptised into Zion.[11] In September 1896, he leased the vacant St Paul's Church and renamed it the Central Tabernacle. Renovations came in at a hefty forty thousand dollars and delivered a state of the art facility with seating for over three thousand people, prayer rooms and a café to accommodate four hundred.[12]

The General Overseer's vision knew no bounds, and his followers seemed happy to support that with their time and money.

Central Tabernacle

According to Dowie, no other church in the world was making "steadier and more rapid progress."[13] He predicted he might be the "the richest person in America" within twenty-five years and would rejoice, "in raising up Zion and in leaving a mighty monument for God in Zion City that will endure until the world is done. That is what I am living for. That is what I am labouring for. That is what I am willing to die for the extension of the glorious Kingdom of God."[14]

If God had blessed his work to date with such bountiful provision, then surely nothing would be impossible for Zion.

WORKING FOR THE KINGDOM

Dowie's ability to inspire his followers to embrace his vision was a key part of his success. From the least to the greatest, everyone had a job to do, and everyone contributed to Zion's mission.

In 1898, the *Zion Seventies* were formed after Dowie heard the story of alcoholic Butch Hutchins, sentenced to death for killing his friend in a drunken stupor. Hutchins' pitiful words, "I never had a chance," deeply disturbed Dowie and he determined never again would anyone in Chicago say that.

The Seventies blanketed Chicago with evangelism, going two-by-two. In one year, covering the city eight times over - a tremendous achievement requiring significant organisation and staying power.[15] They cooked meals, visited the sick, gave out food, clothing and personal invitations to Zion churches.

Jennie Paddock ran the *Zion Home of Hope for Erring Women*. In its first year, the Home of Hope rescued fifty-four women and seven babies from the streets.[16] Zion Publishing expanded their portfolio to produce *The Coming City* (renamed *The Zion Banner*) and the monthly magazine *A Voice from Zion*. These publications were fundraisers and evangelism tools in the hands of the Seventies. Alongside that, the free literature ministry sent out five thousand rolls of print from Zion Publishing every week across the world.[17]

Dowie's social concern was now a driving force for change in Chicago, and the authorities showed him a new respect, unthinkable during the early days of Zion Tabernacle. Doors opened for him in an unprecedented way. In 1895, second-class postal privileges for *Leaves of Healing* were revoked by the Chicago Postmaster who took offence at Dowie's statements on Papal infallibility. But in 1897, Dowie was welcomed by U.S. Postmaster General, William Wilson and successfully lobbied for reinstatement of the discounted postage rate.[18]

While there, he showed Wilson the *Chicago Dispatch*, a seedy newspaper that advertised brothels and enjoyed reduced postage rates. His actions led to editor Joseph Dunlop convicted of sending obscene material through the post and imprisoned for twenty-one months. The *Dispatch* folded when Dunlop was in prison.[19]

Through the meeting with Wilson, Dowie met the Attorney General, who in turn arranged a meeting with President McKinley. Dowie told McKinley he would pray for him, an offer the President gratefully accepted.[20]

Yet more ventures were added under the Zion banner. Zion schools, a Ministry training college and a residential facility for working young women. Churches were planted across Chicago - Zion Tabernacle (South Side); the Bohemian Zion Tabernacle; Zion Tabernacle (West Side) and Zion Tabernacle (North Side).

By 1899, Dowie could boast Zion was now "a mother of churches,"[21] with a presence in Canada, Europe, Scandinavia, Africa and China. And for Dowie, the most exciting development of all. The dream of a golden city that had long been in his heart was now within sight. In preparation, Zion Bank and Zion Land and Investment Association were added to the Zion portfolio.[22]

"I WILL SEND MY MESSENGER"

Astounding progress had been made. But in Dowie's mind, there was so much more to do. His mission statement for Zion in 1899 was an uncompromising 'Go Forward' –

> *Go Forward, O Zion*
> *Great will be thy triumph when the King shall come*
> *Go Forward, O Zion*
> *Thou shalt be exalted when the King shall come.*[23]

Everyone needed to put their hand to the plough and get involved. They must go forward!

It was all going so well. But the pace of ministry took a terrible toll on John Alexander Dowie. If there was ever a Part 1 and Part 2 of his life, consider us moving to Part 2 now. What might once have been a whispered prayer in the night, now took the form of an official announcement.

On 5 March 1899, Dowie declared himself the *Messenger of the Covenant* - the first of a series of prophetic titles he took for himself. The Messenger announcement was a huge leap in the dark, devoid of wisdom and fraught with problems. Dowie was now the living embodiment of Zion.[24] Did he open the door to demonic attack with the Messenger announcement? Perhaps. But Dowie had shown worrying personality traits for much of his ministry. A genuine vision empowered him, but he didn't deal with his flesh.

For all his many successes, divine healing was his gifting. With the Messenger announcement, Dowie tragically stepped into a calling that was not for him, nor indeed for any other mortal being. Nothing good could happen after that and from that time forward, history shows the steady downward trajectory of this great man of God. His anointing remained, but his flesh came to the fore and muted the good thing God put in him.

HOLY WAR

The Holy War on Chicago was the immediate outworking of the new prophetic mandate. In true Malachi style, Dowie's War was against "sorcerers and against the adulterers and against false swearers and against those that oppress the hireling in his wages, the widow and the fatherless and those that turn aside the stranger from his right and fear, not the Lord of Hosts" (Malachi 3.5).

But when making his appeal for funds for the Holy War, an altogether different Dowie was on display from the man who once said that his church was open to all. According to Dowie, the apostles were rich because everyone in Jerusalem sold their homes and gave them their money.[25] By his calculation, "the apostolic treasury" held the equivalent of two hundred and fifty million dollars.[26]

ZION'S HOLY WAR

Program for Sunday, December 3, 1899

THE REV. JOHN ALEX.

DOWIE

GENERAL OVERSEER OF

WILL DELIVER ADDRESSES AS FOLLOWS:

West Side Zion Tabernacle.
Corner Madison and Paulina Streets.
Morning, 10:30—"Zion's Witness Against Those Who Leave God Out."

Central Zion Tabernacle.
1621-1633 Michigan Avenue.
Afternoon, 3:00—"Zion's Cry in the Midnight Hour."
To be followed by Reception of New Members,
Ordination of New Officers and Ordinance of Lord's Supper.

South Side Zion Tabernacle.
6426-6434 Wentworth Avenue.
Evening, 7:45—"What Shall I Do With Jesus?"

COMING EVENTS.

Zion's Witness Against an Unclean, Ungodly and Criminal Press.

Dr. Dowie is preparing a Terrific Indictment and Exposure of the Secular and So-called Religious Press of Chicago, and will deliver a Series of Addresses from December 10th to the 22d, on that subject, in all the Zion Tabernacles of the city.

The First Address will be in Central Zion Tabernacle on Lord's Day, December 10th, at 3:00 P. M. Subject:

"WHO CONTROLS THE NEWSPAPERS, GOD OR THE DEVIL?"

That meant if he needed money, his followers had to give it to him. Dowie warned anyone who did not pay in, "I do not want your company in the Church of God because you will be a curse to us. God's Word has said, plainly, 'Ye are cursed with a curse: for ye rob me.'"[27]

They would be "burned up" and their children with them. The children would be saved in Heaven because they were innocent, but of no use in this world since they were "a bad breed" and it would be better if they had never been born.[28] Whether this was mostly bluster to raise money for down-payments on Zion land is debatable. Certainly, there was no apparent reason why the Holy War - which in effect was a series of sermons preached by Dowie - required such arm-twisting money raising techniques. But surprisingly there did not appear to be too many dissensions, even with this type of dubious scriptural exposition.

Curses aside - the War was motivated by factors that had little to do with Malachi. Firstly, as a distraction for the church when there were already murmurs of discontent on Dowie's stewardship of Zion's money. George Armor Fair, Overseer in Philadelphia, accused Dowie of mismanagement of the Land Association funds and was swiftly removed from his post.[29]

Dowie assured his followers their money was safe with him. He asked Deacons Judd, Sloan and Barnard to swear publicly not a dollar was sidelined for Dowie's personal use.[30] They did - but later events would call that testimony into question.[31]

Secondly, Dowie's agents were covertly concluding deals on the land site for Zion. By diverting the attention of the Chicago newspapers onto the Holy War, he mitigated against the landowners discovering he was behind the land purchase and pushing their prices up.

Thirdly, the Board of Health were actively campaigning to have children taken out of the exemption given to faith healing in the 1899 Medical Practice Act. Dowie wanted to show the "State Board of Death" and the doctors were the murderers, not him. He had a list of abortionists in Chicago and would use it "to put the rope around the neck of fifty of them before I am through."[32]

The Holy War gave him the public platform to take the doctors on.

LAUNCHING THE WAR

He fired the opening shots of the offensive on 8 October 1899 at the launch of two new Zion churches – West Side Tabernacle in the morning and the North Side Tabernacle in the evening.[33]

Dowie went looking for a fight, and the local medical students were happy to oblige. When the student committee of Rush Medical College discovered he would speak on "Doctors Drugs and Devils" at the West Side Tabernacle on 18 October, they put out a call to give him a "hot reception."

An estimated two thousand students turned up. When the service began, hundreds strategically seated in the front rows began to bombard Dowie with stink bombs. [34]

The police intervened, and their attitude stood in stark contrast to their previous animosity. Chief of Police, John D. Shea announced, "He has the right of free speech and should not be mobbed. He pays for the hall used by him, and he is entitled to all the protection the police can give him."[35]

Despite the police assistance on 27 October at Hammond things took a turn for the worse when a riot led to many in the church suffering severe injuries.[36] On Halloween, Dowie was again in Oak Park, and medical students staged yet another invasion.[37] This time round, he was trapped in the church, until the police rescued him.

136

These attacks led to the formation of the Zion Guard – two hundred uniformed men, committed to defending Dowie. It all played to the sense of Zion at war with the hostile world. Everybody knew then that the Devil wasn't happy with Zion.

WAR ON TORREY AND MOODY

Dowie was nothing if not a fighter. He was right to point to the hypocrisy of the Board of Health who attacked him while turning a blind eye to the backstreet abortionists.

Notwithstanding that, there were though uncomfortable aspects to his personality that lay buried under his all-consuming sense of righteous anger. Part of his strategy during the Holy War was to prove he was not the only minister who prayed for divine healing for children. He wanted to show that 'respectable' clergymen also shared his views.

This tactic led to an all-out confrontation with R.A. Torrey, D.L. Moody's associate. Torrey also believed in divine healing. In March 1898 his daughter was ill and might have been saved, but he didn't call a doctor until it was too late. Sadly, she died of diphtheria.

Four weeks later, another daughter lay sick of the same disease. Understandably distraught, Torrey wrote to ask Dowie to come and pray, adding, "You may if you like, read this letter publicly. I believe I have dishonoured the Lord and would be glad to have people know the failure was not in him but in me."[38]

The timeline shows Dowie was out of town and Torrey's second daughter recovered without his intervention. But Dowie kept Torrey's letter, and when accused of child endangerment, he published it in *Leaves of Healing*. Torrey's name associated with Dowie proved too much for the Reverend Frank De Witt Talmage, who demanded Torrey renounce both Dowie and divine healing. According to Talmage, Dowie was a "monumental fraud", and the authorities must step in for "the protection of your children and mine."[39] He told the *Evening Times*,

> Dr Torrey never sent for a physician until the morning his baby was choking to death. Could you dream of a good father guilty of such an awful crime? Then practically writing on the coffin of this dead child, he wrote a letter to Dr Dowie telling him another child was sick with the same awful disease (diphtheria), that Mrs Torrey and he wanted Dowie to come and pray over the child and see if he could find any sin in the parents.[40]

The public attacks shocked the reserved Torrey. To his credit, he responded that, though he still believed in divine healing, he had the greatest respect for doctors and did not agree with Dowie's denunciation of them as "Devils."[41]

Talmage's intervention did not go as planned. Torrey was a well-respected minister, with both the press and public on his side. The *Tribune* reported, "Mr Torrey has been dragged into the affair by the scalp-lock."[42] The *Missouri Valley Times* got straight to the point when they commented the difference between Torrey and Talmage was that one believed in prayer and the other did not. They found it surprising that a "professed Christian clergyman" (Talmage) denounced belief in prayer as "a crime."[43]

D.L. Moody was deeply disturbed at the revelations but nevertheless came to Torrey's defence. He claimed he also believed in divine healing but would call a doctor if he were ill.[44] Dowie hit back at Moody, ridiculing him as yesterday's man. Thousands came to hear him in the past; now he couldn't fill a church! According to Dowie, Moody was "a fool" who had brought sickness into his life.[45]

The Holy War was rapidly descending into an ungainly combat between Dowie and other clergymen, rather than the Devil. Moody died on 22 December 1899, with his last days on earth marred by Dowie's acid attacks. According to Dowie, "It was time that Dwight L. Moody died. God saw he had outlived his usefulness."[46]

"Friends," he told Central Zion Tabernacle, "I can stand anything upon God's earth better than hypocrisy and lies."[47] In such a confrontation, it was "a fight unto death." Torrey would also die if he did not repent.[48] He had "sold his Lord for pieces of silver. He sold his principles for a place and a piece of bread, the coward, the liar, who has robbed God of his glory and curses the Institute with his presence."[49]

Torrey didn't repent, as he didn't see he had done anything to repent of. He retorted that Dowie took his words out of context and invented fictitious material to discredit him. He told the *Tribune*, "Mr Dowie slanders outrageously and deliberately, faithful servants of God."[50]

While this brutal and unedifying confrontation went on, Dowie and his wife kept quiet on their secret sorrow. Throughout their time in America, both Jeanie and Dowie steadfastly maintained their children did not take medicine or see doctors and were none the worse for it. They were remarkably unforthcoming on the sad truth that one of their children died of illness during the height of Dowie's divine healing ministry in Australia.[51] Hardly wrong in itself to want to forget the pain of their dead child - but shoddy and disingenuous, given the so-called fight against "hypocrisy."

The ill-conceived Holy War only receded when Dowie's sights fixed on the fulfilment of his long cherished ambition – Zion, the city of God.

11 GOD'S OWN CITY

ZION CITY.

"Heaven is both a place and a condition."
John Alexander Dowie

DOWIE WAS NOT THE first to dream of building an ideal city. Robert Owen created his secular New Harmony in Indiana back in the 1820s.[1] The Mormons built their own communities with 'Zion' figuring large as the ideal community of the righteous.[2]

But in keeping with Dowie's eschatological focus, Zion was to be different - the launching pad for others cities of Zion across the world.[3] Dowie believed through the establishment of these cities, the church would evangelise the world with a gospel that "had not been preached since apostolic days."[4] For as the Scripture promised, "My cities through prosperity shall yet be spread abroad and the Lord shall yet comfort Zion and shall yet choose Jerusalem.[5]

He reckoned it could be done within twenty-five years.[6] Jerusalem would be bought with Zion's dollars, and then the Lord would come.[7]

SPIES IN THE LAND

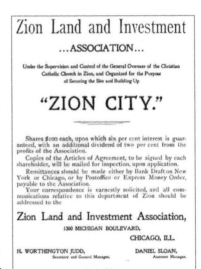

Zion City, Illinois, may well have remained a pipe dream, had it not been for the powerful team Dowie assembled around him.

Burton J. Ashton, a respected civil engineer, responsible for assessing the suitability of the land for development. Charles Barnard, former Chief Clerk of the Commercial National Bank of Chicago and now head of Zion finances. H. Worthington Judd, heading up the Zion Land Association with Daniel Sloan as his second in command. Dr John Speicher, a former theology student and homoeopathic doctor. And respected Chicago lawyer, Samuel Ware Packard.

Packard was the exception in the group, as he didn't join Dowie's church. Notwithstanding that, his trust in Dowie was implicit and his shrewd legal mind behind much of the early Dowie success story.

The search had been on for land for Zion City since 1894, but frustratingly site after site surveyed proved unsuitable. Finally, a

142

large tract of land was identified that might just be right for them.[8] It sat forty-two miles from Chicago and stretched four miles back from Lake Michigan towards Denton. Worthington Judd and Sloan from the Land Division clandestinely visited and came back thrilled at what they saw. Ashton's inspection confirmed the land was more than suitable for development, with the Chicago and Northwestern Railroad running through it.[9]

Dowie was elated and engaged estate agent E.D. Wheelock to negotiate unobtrusively with the landowners for what amounted to a one hundred and fifteen separate plots. By the end of 1899, with the contracts signed, Zion was ready to come out of Dowie's dreams and onto the map of Illinois!

ZION COMES DOWN

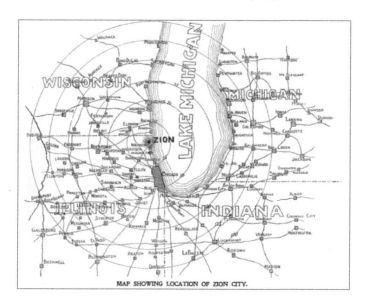

MAP SHOWING LOCATION OF ZION CITY.

At the Watchnight service of 1899, a huge screen hung suspended from the ceiling in Zion Central Tabernacle. On the stroke of midnight, Dowie drew back a curtain and revealed a large map,

143

showing the site of Zion. The map slid away, uncovering an artist's impression of Zion. At the centre rose the dome of the Temple. This was to be the city of God.

From the grandeur of eschatological expectation to the allure of a healthy profit margin, the Zion planners had thought of everything. Samuel Packard told the gathering if they only purchased a small tract of land for Zion City, the farmers would push up their price after Zion people developed it and needed more land.

But they had pulled off a sharp business deal for the property, and it came with a sizable eighty-five percent of the price deferred for three years and no liability to pay taxes.[10] With a locked-in rate, when the mortgages were due, they would buy it at an average price of $157 an acre and sell it to others for thousands of dollars an acre!

Dowie cut into Packard's presentation joking; "Now you have given away where the money is going to come from. You are

144

showing where the millions are coming from and I will soon have no secrets!"[11] Peals of laughter rang out across the hall. Nobody doubted that the money would be there in three years' time to pay off the debt.

Zion Land Investments offered up shares with 6% dividends. Shareholders did not need to become residents of Zion but would be given the first choice in the selection of lots. The city would "make all of the public improvements necessary in establishing a large, clean and enterprising modern city."[12] Industry was planned, educational facilities, a beach and parks for recreation.

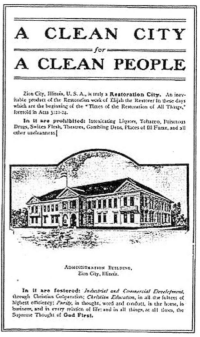

A CLEAN CITY
for
A CLEAN PEOPLE

Zion City, Illinois, U. S. A., is truly a **Restoration City.** An inevitable product of the Restoration work of Elijah the Restorer in these days which are the beginning of the "Times of the Restoration of All Things," foretold in Acts 3:21-24.

In it are prohibited: Intoxicating Liquors, Tobacco, Poisonous Drugs, Swine Flesh, Theatres, Gambling Dens, Places of Ill Fame, and all other uncleanness.

ADMINISTRATION BUILDING,
Zion City, Illinois.

In it are fostered: *Industrial and Commercial Development,* through Christian Coöperation; *Christian Education,* in all the fulness of highest efficiency; *Purity,* in thought, word and conduct, in the home, in business, and in every relation of life; and in all things, at all times, the Supreme Thought of God First.

And to preserve the purity of the city, plots could only be leased, not bought outright. Contracts would forbid gambling, dancing, swearing, spitting, theatres, circuses, the manufacture and sale of alcohol or tobacco, pork, oysters, doctors and politicians. Those who didn't comply would not be welcome. For above all else, Zion was to be "a clean city for a clean people."

THE BEAUTIFUL DREAM

On 22 February 1900, the first band of pilgrims set foot on Zion's sacred soil when a party of several hundred "saw its beautiful terraces and groves and meadows for the first time."[13]

JOHN ALEXANDER DOWIE – A HELPER OF MEN

They needed a fair bit of imagination because at that point the only evidence 'Zion' was any different from the surrounding farmland, was some narrow plank sidewalk and the optimistically-named "Zion Observatory Tower" which stood at the centre of the Zion Temple site in Shiloh Park.[14]

Could they actually turn this undeveloped farmland into the city of God? No one seemed to doubt it. Yet it was a huge step for Dowie's followers to give up their personal freedoms and live under Dowie's authority. For, "Everyone who knew Zion, knew that Dowie was Zion."[15]

The people of Zion didn't see it that way. They thought they were the chosen ones - the first of the one hundred and forty and four thousand who would be selected from among Zion cities to judge the earth.[16]

And, on the face of it, Zion was indeed a lucrative offer of Heaven come down. "God forbid," said Dowie, "that we should refuse citizenship in God's Zion on earth to a single citizen of the Heavenly Zion. Neither race, nor colour not education, nor position, nor wealth can be a barrier to fellowship."[17] Hard work would produce results for all, with profits going to God, workers and shareholders alike.

There would be no Rockefellers in Zion for what man earned fifty million dollars honestly?[18] Zion would be ruled by God because "where God rules, man prospers."[19] It would lead the way in adopting new models for doing church that flew in the face of conventional wisdom and righted the injustices of society. Discrimination and prejudice had no part in God's city.

Women were treated as equals with Dowie proclaiming it was

146

"a perfect abomination that a woman should get less than a man because she is a woman."[20]

Children were valued and encouraged in their education.[21] And in a nation still fraught with racial division, Faupel noted, "One Negro visitor observing the conditions of his fellow Blacks stated that Dr Dowie must be 'the most courageous man in the nation."[22]

Everyone had a place, and everyone mattered. It was the gospel in action, and the beautiful dream goes a long way to explaining why thousands of people were willing to give their money and their lives over to Dowie. They belonged. They were part of the Kingdom of God in Zion.

CHILDREN OF THE HEAVENLY KING

Of course, it wasn't only about social change and world mission. The heady mixture undoubtedly included elements of hero worship of Dowie. However, Rolvix Harlan's claim that Zion residents were "weak-framed, dull-witted creatures"[23] is unsubstantiated.

Harlan wrote one of the first studies on Zion in 1906. His work, though well-researched as a whole, illustrates the prejudice that manifestly existed against Dowie's followers at that time. A large group of people who come together and within only a few years, build a city worth millions of dollars on undeveloped land with its police force, laws, education and industry are hardly "dim-witted." On the contrary, they appear very resourceful.

So who were the children of the Heavenly King in Zion?

There is a range of views amongst commentators on Dowie. Philip Cook believed the bulk of Dowie's followers were middle-class Protestants. For Cook, Zion was a particularly American phenomenon that combined Christian idealism with the sanctification of riches that characterised the American dream.[24]

By way of contrast, Grant Whacker noted many of Dowie's followers were healed under his ministry. Wacker suggested these healings were seen as the tangible symbol of a release from sin - "Healing represented not only a release from pain but also a sacrament, a palpable symbol of those rare but unforgettable moments of grace in the life of the believer."[25]

And for Gordon Lindsay, who was born in Zion, the attraction of the city was both social and religious - the ideal city to bring up children in a holy lifestyle. A place where it was easy to do good and hard to do bad.[26]

These insights are probably all correct in their own way. The same thing doesn't motivate everyone, and a broad group of people from different backgrounds were happy to follow Dowie to Zion. They gave up jobs, farms, businesses and said goodbye to family and friends. For better or worse, their futures were now wrapped up with John Alexander Dowie.

The eschatological dimension is perhaps less tangible but still a powerful motivating factor behind the desire to move to Zion. Dowie's followers genuinely believed they were on the cusp of a great moment in history and that infused the venture with a sense of destiny and grandeur. These were the sons and daughters of generations of immigrants who travelled to the shores of America, looking for their Heaven on earth.

Now their moment had come - the prelude to that great cataclysmic moment in time when "the end will come when he hands over the kingdom to God the Father after he has destroyed all dominion, authority and power" (1 Corinthians 15:24).

BUILDING ZION

So it was a solemn but joyous crowd who gathered again on 14 July 1900 to consecrate the site of Zion Temple with the Observatory Tower at its centre, decked out in flags. Arthur Newcomb, present amongst the two thousand gathered there that day, captured the mood of the moment when he wrote,

> It was a day fraught with the mightiest significance to
> Zion and to the world. It was a day the power of
> which will grow and extend as the days and the years
> go by until, as each succeeding anniversary rolls
> around, entire nations will mark its passage with
> joyous convocations and songs of praise to God.[27]

Dowie told them that they were now in the *Times of Restoration* - "The Restoration of the Church; the Restoration of the Home; the Restoration of the State."[28] With this would come the restoration of all nine gifts of the Spirit. They would not be restored to an apostate church, but only to Zion, the true church of God.[29] Zion Temples would rise around the world and "would send their representatives to the glorious Temple at Jerusalem when Christ our King shall come."[30]

Suitably stirred by this rousing word, processions from the uniformed Zion Guards, Junior and Senior Seventies marched three times around the Temple site, waving flags and singing,

Then let our songs abound
And every tear be dry
We're marching thro' Immanuel's ground
To fairer worlds on high.

We're marching to Zion
Beautiful, beautiful Zion
We're marching upward to Zion
The beautiful City of God.

Samuel Packard, on behalf of the business cabinet, presented a silver spade to Dowie and to rapturous applause, he turned over the first shovel of dirt on the site of the Temple. In the afternoon, he preached on the glorious future of Zion. Around the Temple would spring up, "colleges, great schools of learning, schools of industry, manual training schools, orphanages, Divine Healing Homes, libraries, places where the people can come and get blessing."[31] Newcomb recalled the sense of wonder that thrilled their hearts as they listened to Dowie's words,

> This little band of a few thousand people saw themselves the favoured instruments in the consummation of the plan of the ages, nucleus of the chosen company of kings and priests of God, which ere long should rule the whole world.[32]

Surely God had come to Zion, Illinois. The golden city was now a reality.

ZION TAKES SHAPE

With the mighty end-time commission behind them, by the end of 1900, the lumberyard was functioning, a blacksmith shop, a freight warehouse and a telegraph office. Conditions were rough and frontier-like, with workers living in tents and temporary shacks. But the ideal city was no random collection of buildings. Zion was planned with prodigious care and designed on exact geometric lines, with two boulevards through the centre, crossed by two avenues at a forty-five-degree angle.

The North and South streets all carried Biblical names, bar Caledonia and Edina, to remind Dowie of his roots. Houses sprang up. Roads were built. Trees planted. Drainage put in. From Aaron Avenue on the lakeshore to Zebulon Avenue four and a half miles inshore, God's own city took shape.

Dowie called himself as "only a business man in the ministry."[33] His own experience of deprivation meant he knew more than most Zion needed to make money to survive. That became his principal focus in the years to come, Lindsay believed, at the cost of his personal anointing.[34]

Many industries were planned, most of them around construction, as could be expected in the early days. But there was also the Candy Factory, the Furniture Store and the General Stores. In the spring of 1900, an important addition joined the Zion family in the shape of English lace-maker Samuel Stevenson. He visited Dowie in 1899 and fell in love with Jeanie Dowie's sister, Mary Ann, also visiting Zion from Australia. They married, with Gladstone Dowie as the best man and Esther Dowie, a bridesmaid.[35]

Deacon Stevenson was now 'family' and afforded the best Zion could offer.[36] He decided to relocate his family and business from England to Zion, including the skilled workers for the factory.[37]

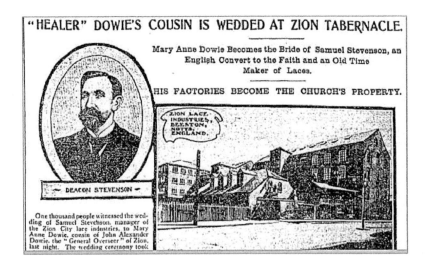

"HEALER" DOWIE'S COUSIN IS WEDDED AT ZION TABERNACLE.

Mary Anne Dowie Becomes the Bride of Samuel Stevenson, an English Convert to the Faith and an Old Time Maker of Laces.

HIS FACTORIES BECOME THE CHURCH'S PROPERTY.

ZION LACE INDUSTRIES, BEESTON, NOTTS, ENGLAND.

– DEACON STEVENSON –

One thousand people witnessed the wedding of Samuel Stevenson, manager of the Zion City lace industries, to Mary Anne Dowie, cousin of John Alexander Dowie, the "General Overseer" of Zion, last night. The wedding ceremony took

Bringing him into the fold was a massive achievement for Dowie, who calculated the Lace Factory could employ fifty thousand people and be worth five million dollars in five years' time.[38] The two men signed a contract in April 1900, and Zion Lace Industries were now in business, with shares priced at $100 and paying dividends of six percent, going up yearly to twelve percent.[39]

With everything moving forward in the city of God, in August 1900 Dowie made ready to leave for Europe with his family and the newly-weds Mary Ann and Samuel Stevenson.

Before they left, there was a little matter of a contract variation to be completed. Dowie's attorney Samuel Packard took care of it with his customary attention to detail, and the wedding party set sail for the old country.

12 ZION
UNCOVERED

"Now here is the king you have chosen, the one you asked for;
see, the Lord has set a king over you."
1 Samuel 12:13

ZION PROMISED BLESSINGS FOR this world and the next, with healthy profits to boot. But both the Bible and church history would call into question the wisdom of this so-called "Theocracy."

Journalist Elbert Hubbard cut to the chase when he wrote, "It is the manifestation of a very old idea - the supremacy of the priest, the temporal power of the pope. Dowie supplies the creed, and he furnishes employment, which is better than the others do. He has his uniformed soldiers to enforce his orders and all who do not obey absolutely have to hike."[1]

Hubbard's sobering words are a good point to reflect on what was happening in Zion, behind all the eschatological fervour. Dowie was not the first, or last, leader to come to power on the back of popular sentiment by promising to restore the glory of a bygone era. His restoration of the "primitive church" was a powerful message to a generation of believers increasingly marginalised by secularisation. Moreover, the miracles accomplished at his hands seemed to put the stamp of Heavenly approval on his vision.

Unfortunately, 'ideal societies' tend to reflect our own ideals. And Christians, of all traditions, are notorious for seeing God's Word through the lens of their cultural perspective and then finding this view 'supported' by the Scripture. Dowie was again, no different. He took capitalist ideals, infused them with a Biblical theme, in a utopian world of his making. In that perfect world, Dowie was accountable to no-one. He was John Alexander – a helper of men. His vision for Zion was bountiful; everyone would be free and equal. At the same time, it was oppressive. They could be free, as long as they conformed to the rules. Dowie's rules.

IRON FIST IN A VELVET GLOVE

The problem was Dowie owned *everything* in Zion. The land their houses were built on - was owned by Dowie. The factories

154

they would work in - were owned by Dowie. The shops they bought their food from - were owned by Dowie. The schools they would send their children to - were owned and controlled by Dowie. The church they were a part of was, in every way, controlled by Dowie.

It's hard to understand why any person would want to have such control over another human being. It was almost a return to medieval serfdom.[2] Although the enormous activity of building Zion provided a distraction to these fatal flaws in the foundations, it didn't take long for the rot to set in. When Zion Bank opened in 1899, Dowie drew upon the Bank's funds to pay off $65,000 of debt and took an average of $84,000 a year for "personal expenses."[3]

Dowie later claimed this was for Zion projects. That may have been true, but refusing to be accountable to anyone except God in the matter of other people's money, was a questionable ethical model.

It was just the beginning of the slow slide down. On the day before his party left for London, Dowie gave Samuel Stevenson a new contract to sign. Stevenson's company was essential for Dowie to attract more people into Zion and he wanted full control over it, as with the other Zion industries. In the new contract, hastily drawn up by Samuel Packard, Stevenson agreed to sign over *all* of his assets to Dowie. Rather than be a partner with Dowie, Stevenson would now be a shareholder in Dowie's company.

MARY DIES

The 'Europe Tour' was unspectacular, bar the riots by medical students who invaded meetings in London. Churches shut their doors to Dowie and his party and baptisms ended up taking place in public baths.[4]

Mary Ann took ill and decided to cut short her trip and go back to America. Meanwhile, Dowie and his family travelled on to Paris to visit the World Fair.

DOWIE'S SISTER IS DEAD.

"BRAVELY REFUSED MEDICAL CARE," HUSBAND SAYS.

Chicago Tribune, 28 November 1900

Sadly, Mary Ann died of pneumonia on the journey home, and Stevenson arrived back in Zion a grieving widower, after burying his wife at sea. She was brave to the end he told everyone, denying all medical treatment.[5]

The workers for the Lace Factory arrived just after Stevenson when Attorney Packard resolved their delays with US immigration.[6]

By then far from just the usual tedium of red tape and bureaucracy, every set-back in Zion was now a battle between light and darkness. On this occasion, Dowie claimed Zion, "put to flight all the hosts of Zion's Labour Union enemies." These Labour union 'devils' questioned the import of foreign labour under the Alien Contract Labour Law.[7]

Stevenson busied himself organising the set-up of the Lace Factory, alongside his two brothers Henry and Arthur. In the rush to promote Zion Lace stock, no actual premises were built as yet, and the machinery went into a temporary structure, awaiting the construction of a permanent brick building.

Back in Europe, Dowie claimed Jeanie was "dangerously prostrated with grief at her sister's departure."[8] So much so, he cancelled a proposed visit to Palestine. When Jeanie questioned him why her sister died, he told her he didn't have all the answers on divine healing, but God had revealed to him it was Samuel Stevenson's fault!

She seemed satisfied with this explanation, and with the additional bonus of being made *Overseer of all the Women's Work in Zion*, Jeanie appeared to have rallied. So much so, she decided to stay on in Paris for six months with Esther to study French and do some shopping.[9]

Jeanie Dowie was a somewhat credulous woman, but she was not to blame for her husband's mistakes. She naively accepted everything he said and had done so for her entire married life since their fall out back in 1877. Despite the barbed remarks on her closets of expensive clothes brought home from Paris,[10] she considered it only right and proper for the General Overseer's wife to dress fitting to her status.

Dowie told her they were rich, so she spent the money. As for Esther, she was an attractive young girl, free for a season from her father's influence in an exciting cosmopolitan city. Who could blame her for wanting to go out, buy new clothes and get the latest hairstyle? He did his best to keep the harsh realities of life away from them, including leaving them behind in France when he went back to face Stevenson.

THE WORM TURNS

On return to Zion, Dowie demanded Stevenson ship more machinery from Yorkshire and hand it over to him. Stevenson refused, and this led to an open breach between the two men in April 1901. The velvet glove came off with Dowie calling Stevenson "a murderer."[11] The Englishman was swiftly removed from his position at the Lace Factory, and his brother Arthur Stevenson put in charge.

Zion Lace Industries
....Incorporated....

JOHN ALEX. DOWIE, *President*   HENRY STEVENSON, *General Manager*
CHAS. J. BARNARD, *Treasurer*   H. WORTHINGTON JUDD, *Secretary*

This Industry, begun in 1901, now occupies a splendid building in Zion City, with five acres of floor space. It is the only factory in America making high-grade machine laces. Its Products include Fancy Laces, Allover Nets, Valenciennes, and Normandy Laces, and Lace Curtains in Nottingham styles and finish. . . . .

The rancorous dispute made Zion jittery. In June 1901, Dowie attempted to calm fears by writing that the "numerous rumours in the press and otherwise, as to mysterious dangers to Zion's Lace Industries are absolutely false." Only one man had, "broken his agreement and gone."[12]

That until only months before, the factory belonged to this "one man" seemed to be unnecessary detail. It belonged to Dowie now, and by the end of September, he could tell the stockholders, "The loss of only one man has not hindered us for a moment, and all is well with Zion Lace Industries."[13]

A few weeks later, the worm turned. Samuel Stevenson called foul and lodged a lawsuit with the Illinois courts, alleging Dowie defrauded him out of his Lace Factory.

DOWIE GOES TO COURT

Until then Dowie's financial affairs, though the subject of intense speculation, had little actual detail made public. *Leaves of Healing* carried glowing accounts of the Lace Factory but would not "enter into details of management or into figures as to production."[14]

Now, with the Stevenson lawsuit in the public domain, Zion's business was on display for the watching world.

Judge Murray F. Tuley heard the case, a respected legal expert with a reputation for ensuring equal access to law for rich and poor. Appearing for Stevenson, Attorney Reeves told the court Dowie "found" Stevenson in England and persuaded him to visit Chicago.[15]

When Stevenson arrived in December 1899, he agreed to sell his factory to Dowie for $50,000 cash and $100,000 fully paid-up stock, in a million dollar incorporated company that Dowie would capitalise.[16] Dowie promised to find him a wife and Stevenson subsequently married Mary Ann Dowie and signed a prenuptial agreement to give $50,000 of his paid-up stock to his new wife, with her brother-in-law as her trustee.

Stevenson was highly satisfied with the arrangement, but things changed when a new agreement reversed the original contract. He claimed Dowie pressured him into signing this, which he did, but without understanding the significance.

THE 'PRIVATE' AGREEMENT'

The new contract had two parts. Under the 'public agreement,' the Lace Factory would not be incorporated, but rather have shares guaranteed only by Dowie. There would be no scrutiny of the finances as the contract stipulated, "the shareholders shall have no right, without express permission first obtained from said, John Alex Dowie, to examine the books of said Zion Lace Industries."[17]

The second part of the contract - the so-called 'private agreement' - stipulated instead of $100,000 fully paid-up stock, Stevenson would receive bonds guaranteed by Dowie to the value of $100,000.[18] And instead of paid-up shares, Mary Ann would receive $50,000 unincorporated bonds.[19] Stevenson was to purchase these bonds by selling more machinery to Dowie for $35,000 cash and the remaining $15,000 would be covered by the balance of money Dowie owed him on the original transaction.[20]

In effect, Stevenson had sold his company to Dowie for nothing, bar interest paying bonds.

Stevenson told the court he mistakenly thought the private agreement was a copy of the public agreement and was not aware he had even signed it until Dowie later produced a copy bearing his signature. Dowie had taken his paperwork for safekeeping before they left for England, and it was not returned to him.

Charles Barnard, in turn, gave testimony that he personally put Stevenson's private agreement in Zion Bank safe after Dowie passed it to him. It disappeared mysteriously and later turned up in Dowie's possession when he demanded more machinery from Stevenson.[21]

Barnard could not account for how the paperwork was removed from the safe and ended up in Dowie's hands.

PACKARD ON TRIAL

Samuel Packard strenuously defended Dowie in court but as he was the witness to the two agreements, that left him incredibly compromised.

While noting the discrepancies in the witnesses' accounts, Tuley remarked Packard was known to the court over many years as a man of integrity and honour. On that basis, he was satisfied no fraud could be contemplated.[22] Yet, Tuley questioned, why did Stevenson, who had a favourable contract from only months before, sign another contract that in effect gave everything he owned over to Dowie?

The Judge agreed with Packard's assessment that Stevenson was no match for Dowie in intelligence or business acumen. Knowing that Tuley questioned, why did Packard not ensure Stevenson had independent legal advice before signing the new contract?[23] By failing to do so, Packard drew up and witnessed a contract that was, "a gift by Stevenson to Dowie of all his property, rights and interests."[24]

According to Tuley, Dowie's sole investment in the Lace Factory was limited to "the credulity of his followers," "their avarice at the profits that could be made," and their "blind faith" in Dowie.[25]

On putting up no more than a "shed" (the temporary structure for the Lace Factory), Dowie raised a staggering $431,000, with absolute control over the money and no-one authorised to scrutinise where the money went.[26]

Tuley then turned his attention to whether Stevenson was

161

under "undue influence" in signing the disputed contract. Stevenson told the court Dowie claimed to be "God's Messenger" recognised by "the sign." Zion residents were in fear of Dowie, as he claimed those who opposed him died.[27]

Excerpts from *Leaves of Healing* appeared to support that view. The court heard Dowie's message on the story of Ananias and Sapphira which concluded those who did not give Dowie money would suffer a similar fate - "…you will die in Zion most surely. I will find you out some day, and if ever I do, that will be the last of you."[28]

When combined with the evidence presented on Dowie's comments on the deaths of D.L. Moody and others who opposed him, it was evident, things did not look good for Zion's leader.[29] Tuley summed up,

> If Dowie believes, as he says he does, in a theocracy, in other words, in a people governed by the immediate direction of the Almighty, like the Israelites of old and his followers also believe the same and that he speaks by the authority of God, can it be said that any one of his followers entering into a contract or business arrangement with John Alexander Dowie is not acting under "undue influence?" The law says that "undue influence" shall be presumed in such a case.[30]

Dowie could not say that he spoke for God and threaten death if his followers didn't obey, then claim people exercised their free will in signing over their assets to him! Tuley told the warring parties he was minded to set aside the agreement of 4 August 1900 and reinstate Stevenson's previous contract. But he would give them until the beginning of January 1902 to reach a deal out of court to avert receivership.[31]

ZION'S INDUSTRIES ILLEGAL

More cases were lodged with Stevenson's attorney from ex-employees who claimed they were sacked because they planned to testify for Stevenson.[32] Attorney Reeves sensed victory and said Stevenson would accept $175,000 cash, nothing less.[33] In turn, Packard offered up $50,000 to compensate for the stock held by Mary Ann Stevenson.[34]

$400,000

Zion Lace Industries

ACCUMULATIVE

Preferred Coupon Stock,

Represented by Certificates with Coupons for the Guaranteed Interest, as well as for the Contingent Dividend.

SHARES $100 EACH

INTEREST PAID AS FOLLOWS:

Guaranteed Interest payable Semi-Annually, and Contingent Interest Annually, at the following rates:

First Year,	6 Per Cent
Second Year,	7 Per Cent
Third Year,	8 Per Cent
Fourth Year,	9 Per Cent
Fifth Year,	10 Per Cent
Sixth Year,	11 Per Cent
Seventh Year,	12 Per Cent

STATEMENT

Estimated area occupied by Industries, 30 to 80 acres.

Estimated number of hands employed at the end of five years, 50,000

Estimated value of property at the end of five years, at least $5,000,000

In view of the fluctuations in the value of stocks listed on Stock Exchanges, caused many times by manipulation of unscrupulous men, we believe the careful investor will appreciate the value of this stock, which cannot be purchased except through this Bank.

ARTICLES OF AGREEMENT MAILED UPON APPLICATION

The arguments dragged on until Tuley wearied of the whole thing and handed down his judgement at the end of January 1902. He said the role of the law was to protect the weak against the oppression of the strong. Dowie had duped Stevenson, and a receiver should be appointed with a bond of $700,000 for the Lace Factory. The legal status of the Factory should be resolved, as it was in breach of the Illinois Law of Perpetuities.[35]

In fact, *all* of Zion's twenty-eight industries were in violation of the same law and Dowie was to give a full list of Zion stock subscribers to the receiver.[36]

Attorney Packard put on a brave face at the defeat and argued, "We did not deny that money was due to Stevenson but we fought the case because the charges made reflected upon Dr Dowie."[37]   Dowie showed no such grace.   Tuley was now, "the arch-enemy of Zion,"[38] a "miserable, malevolent, wicked, unjust Judge."[39]

Despite the prophetic denunciations and name-calling, Dowie settled quickly out of court for an undisclosed sum, reputed to be in the region of $200,000, to mitigate against further damage to Zion assets.

The wily Dowie's financial sleight of hand had backfired badly on Zion, and Samuel Stevenson was now rich beyond his wildest dreams.

OVER-CAPITALISED

Packard persuaded Dowie that although the judgement on the legality of Zion's industries was not legally binding, they needed to move quickly to incorporate the Lace Factory.

In truth, little changed. Dowie boasted, "Judge Tuley said we should become a corporation. We did so. I am the corporation."[40]

Three years later, Henry Stevenson told Rolvix Harlan the Lace Factory was *three times* over-capitalised, but with insufficient funds to buy enough raw material to maintain full production. It had only eighteen machines, but the capacity for eighty-two. Despite all the money ploughed in, it never made a profit.

He said when he questioned the lack of capital with the leaders at Zion Bank, "They told me to mind my own business, and they would attend to theirs."[41]   Stevenson's complaints saw him removed from his position but kept on full salary to stop him from suing Dowie.[42]

If Stevenson's statements were correct - and subsequent events seem to back them up - he indicated collusion in the Dowie inner circle to cover up financial mismanagement, even at this early stage. Wilbur Voliva later alleged in court in 1906, supported by Zion's leaders, that Dowie syphoned off a staggering 1.4 million dollars from Zion Lace Factory for personal expenditure.[43]

CLEAN GOTTEN MONEY

It is scarcely credible so much money could go missing, and nobody noticed it. But the people of Zion seemed to see pretty much what they wanted to see.

To assist that process on 9 February 1902, Dowie delivered a stinging rebuttal of Stevenson and Tuley in "Hear What the Unjust Judge Saith" and as part of that paraded Arthur and Henry Stevenson on stage to denounce their brother as a liar.[44]

That seemed to placate most of Dowie's followers without overly worrying about the detail. Many of them had shares in Zion industries, and their dividends could be in jeopardy if Samuel Stevenson caused ructions.

Dowie told them he settled out of court to protect their interests. That was good enough for them. And they were happy to give a hearty "Amen" to his prayer offered after his lengthy denunciation of the "liar Stevenson" and the "unjust Judge" -

> Help us with clean gotten money to do thy work in establishing schools and colleges; in sending out thy messengers; in feeding the hungry; in clothing the naked; in bringing the Glad Tidings of Salvation, Healing and Holy Living through Faith in Jesus to all Nations of the Earth. For this purpose, we are in business for thee, O God.[45]

If Judge Tuley could not save the people of Zion from their 'blind faith' in Dowie, God himself would need to do it.

13 ELIJAH MUST COME

"O wad some Pow'r the giftie gie us,
To see oursels as others see us,
It wad frae monie a blunder free us, An' foolish notion."
Robert Burns

THE PEOPLE OF ZION believed God had chosen their leader for an incredible purpose and destiny.

They equated Dowie with God and anyone who spoke against him with the Devil. They had given Dowie their money, their time and now they were prepared to give him their minds.

They were satisfied that whatever he said the Bible meant, that was what it meant. Even if it contradicted something, he said sometime before.[1] To live in a 'Theocracy' meant God was in control of their lives, with Dowie, the man who spoke for him.

And as if to underline his God-given authority to rule over them in June 1901, Dowie announced himself as *Elijah the Restorer*.

"I am Elijah the prophet who appeared first as Elijah himself, second as John the Baptist and who now comes in me, the restorer of all things. Elijah was a prophet, John was a preacher, but I combine in myself the attributes of prophet, priest and ruler over men."[2]

> **DOWIE CLAIMS DIVINE POSITION,**
>
> ———
>
> Says He Is Raised Up as Ruler of Men, Messenger of the Covenant.
>
> ———
>
> **HERE IN FORM OF ELIJAH.**
>
> ———
>
> Strangers in Crowd at Auditorium Leave Aghast at the Overseer's Words.
>
> ———
>
> **TALKS OF HAVING KINGDOM.**
>
> **Chicago Tribune, 3 June 1901**

Dowie was no longer subject to man since Jesus had, "committed the world to his charge as the forerunner of the millennium, the one who would hasten its coming."[3]

Such a momentous revelation was bound to come as a surprise to many, even those steeped in the Dowie hyperbole. In the history of the world, God had chosen no other mortal being for such a task.

Yet a staggering three thousand people stood in Central Tabernacle in agreement with Dowie's claim, including many who would go on and form the early Pentecostal movement.

Evil triumphs, as the maxim goes, when good men do nothing. Dowie had many good men and women, around him but none who tempered his "foolish notion" that he was the Prophet Elijah. According to Lindsay it became "a fixation" and his guiding light,

> He utterly believed that as a fulfilment of prophecy, God raised him up to bring about a restoration of worldwide extent, of all things spoken by the prophets. This if true, actually involved and anticipated nothing more or less than a dispensational change in God's dealing with the human race.[4]

For Lindsay, it was, "Satan's master scheme to interrupt the work that God really gave him to do."[5]

THE DIVINE COMMISSION

The 'Elijah Declaration' came as part of a tirade at Dowie's old foe, Commissioner Reynolds of the Board of Health. Reynolds wanted Zion Home registered as a hospital. Dowie countered it was a hotel and many hotels in Chicago had resident doctors but didn't register as hospitals.[6] Besides he wasn't subject to man – he was Elijah!

He told the Central Tabernacle that he didn't discuss the revelation of his Elijah ministry with anyone, including his wife. It was a divine commission,[7] but not altogether a surprise to him. Many years before in Adelaide, a dying Jewish woman told him emphatically, "You are Elijah!"

Her words stopped Dowie in his tracks. Could it be true? Was he really the one to bring in the Times of Restoration?

I wept, stood and wept in my heart. Thump!
Thump! Thump! Were the words - "You are Elijah!"
Why did you not tell her you have come? I resented
it and said, "I am not."[8]

According to Dowie, the woman died because she "would not
confess Christ."[9] In the years to follow, others brought similar
words to him, but he didn't accept them either. Yet hadn't John
the Baptist said, "I am not" when people questioned him if he was
Elijah? Dowie had done likewise, but now he was prepared to
accept the divine call upon his life.

THE RESTORATION OF ALL THINGS

In effect, the Elijah Declaration didn't add a great deal to Dowie's
prophetic mandate to date – namely the restoration of the now
mythical concept he called "the primitive church."[10]

For Dowie, Jesus was coming soon. Elijah must come to
restore all things before the Second Coming of Christ. He was
doing the works of Elijah, so he must be Elijah and his ministry,
"the beginning of the Restoration of All Things" -

> The Times prophesied by the early apostles of the
> primitive Christian Church have come. The Times
> which saints and martyrs and holy men of God in all
> the ages have foreseen and looked forward to with
> intensest longing have come.[11]

Against the backdrop of this enormous shift in God's dealings
with the world, it followed that belief in Dowie as Elijah was not
optional for Zion's leaders. Either they accepted the revelation,

or they got out.[12] Outside of Zion, the Elijah Declaration was met first with incredulity, then outright hostility. Undaunted, Dowie countered, "the mere sullen denial" of the facts proved nothing.[13] He had thousands of witnesses to prove the validity of his mission.

He was Elijah, whether they believed it or not. According to Dowie, "All Zion knew I was the prophet before I announced it and I had hard, work keeping them from exploiting the fact before I was ready. Like John the Baptist, I was not sure of myself until a strange light appeared unto me."[14]

FADING ANOINTING

Hindsight suggests the "strange light" was more likely the product of his over-worked mind than a revelation from God.[15]

Dowie was under incredible pressure to maintain the empire he built. He relied on his personal charisma to obtain large sums of money from his followers, and he was extremely successful in that, but it was hardly the most robust business model.

To compound matters, the obsession with being seen to succeed diverted his attention from a focus on his gifting in divine healing. *Leaves of Healing* once burst with accounts of 'God's Witnesses to Divine Healing' but now featured a new case sporadically, with re-runs of previous stories and pictures of Dowie, Jeanie and the other Zion leaders filling the gaps.

Could Jeanie have brought some focus back to him? Unlikely. After their fallout in 1877, Jeanie seems to have taken a backseat in their relationship and now contented herself with numerous photo opportunities, foreign holidays and shopping.

On return from her extended stay in Paris, Jeanie told her Zion ladies, speculation on the Second Coming should be avoided. People like the General Overseer and other teachers knew about it but salvation, holiness and healing mattered most. The rest was of inferior importance, "principally, theories and wordy speculations."[16]

Two weeks later, her husband announced he was Elijah. A revelation that must have taken even Jeanie by surprise. But one she seemed to take in her stride.

THE BIG SALE

Dowie was nothing if not the master of choosing the moment of his prophetic revelations. As the Messenger revelation preceded the Holy War, the Elijah announcement came just weeks before the official opening of Zion City on 15 July 1901.

Sales of land plots were not going as quickly as expected and a new offer of a "limited" number of plots would close at "an early date."[17] Worthington Judd and Sloan advised investors to "secure stock at once,"[18] while Attorney Packard estimated Dowie could make fifteen million dollars at the "big sale."[19]

With Elijah II making a personal appearance at the Land Sale

172

Tent, the pageantry that came to characterise Zion sprang into action. From all across America, pilgrims pitched their tents at the Camp of Esther for the Feast of Tabernacles.

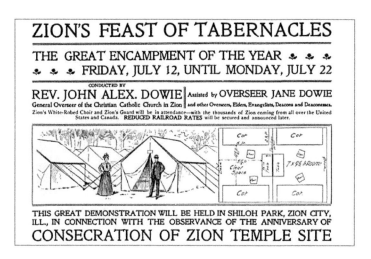

It all served to reinforce the sense of the sacred journey away from the corrupt world to the Heavenly city on the shores of Lake Michigan. And although the fifteen million dollars didn't materialise, by December 1901 the *Zion Banner* could claim they had gone from undeveloped farmland to,

> "A City of from 3000 to 4000 inhabitants, stores, markets, mills, factories, passenger and freight depots, schools, a bank, a hospice, streets and sidewalks."[20]

Shiloh Tabernacle, the focus point of community life, was completed in April 1902. It could accommodate eight thousand worshippers, with room for a choir of five hundred.

Dowie's three-storey home Shiloh House, extended to an impressive twenty rooms. It cost ninety thousand dollars to build, with an additional forty thousand spent on a well-stocked library.[21] These were huge sums of money, given the average wage in Zion amounted to only ten to fifteen dollars a week.[22]

But the people of Zion didn't grudge a little luxury to their leader. They thought it only right and proper that Dowie lived in the manner befitting his status in the community and entertaining his many visitors.

Shiloh House

THE RUBICON CROSSED

In his newfound prophetic role, Dowie proved more vitriolic than ever. By May 1902 he had preached thirty-five *Elijah Restoration* messages, taking to task anyone and everyone who opposed his views.[23]

As far as he was concerned, God had set him apart to put the world right and as Lindsay put it, "the Rubicon was crossed. There could be no retracing of his steps."[24]

But as he pushed forward relentlessly, tragedy again struck the Dowie family in the spring of 1902. Esther Dowie boarded at Zion Home while a student at Chicago University. Her father was out of town and, in his absence, she agreed to host Percy Booth-Clibborn, the son-in-law of Salvation Army founder General Booth.[25]

It was no sin to want to look her best - but it took Esther

Dowie's life. A forbidden alcohol lamp, perched on her dressing table for curling irons, accidentally fell over and set her clothes alight. She screamed for help, but her locked bedroom door held back those who came running. A gust of wind from an open window fanned the flames and sealed Esther's fate. Her body was scorched "to a crisp" with seventy-five percent burns.[26]

Esther Dowie

Dowie rushed back to Chicago and spent a grief-stricken day with his daughter. She died of shock within twelve hours.[27]

Without a doubt, Esther's death broke Dowie's heart. His last surviving daughter, now gone. But not even the awfulness of losing his "Princess" could shake him in his convictions. She disobeyed, so she died. He preached at her funeral, attended by hundreds of grieving friends, "The devil struck her with that 'liquid fire and distilled damnation.'" One blow and she was gone.[28]

PACKARD DEFECTS

Trouble was not over for Dowie. After many years of loyal support, somewhat incongruously Samuel Packard cut all ties with Dowie in August 1902. He joined Zion only a few weeks before, then suddenly withdrew his membership and returned to his former Congregational Church in Oak Park.

Packard wouldn't discuss the reasons for his defection but said it was by mutual agreement.[29] Mrs Packard's refusal to move to

Zion and reluctance to hand over their money to Dowie was rumoured to be behind the decision.[30]

V.V. Barnes replaced Packard, leaving behind a Chicago law practice to become Zion City attorney. Shortly after his arrival, he was in court defending Dowie against the executors of the estate of Mary Tindall who had invested her considerable fortune in Zion. Daniel Sloan gave evidence that Zion City was sound and a good investment.[31]

But, as the unpaid bills mounted up, it must surely have been apparent to Zion's leaders, far from being "sound", Zion City was in severe financial difficulty.

Dowie's behaviours became increasingly more dictatorial and erratic. He told his followers they had no right to expect a miracle unless they were prepared to stand by him a hundred percent. Obedience to Dowie must be absolute, or persecution would follow,

> It were better for you that you had never been born than that you should start out to fight Elijah. I will defeat you every time.[32]

To emphasise his point, Dowie used the example of Esther's death. She only disobeyed once, but that was enough. She died. It was a sin unto death,

> Apply the Lesson. If my daughter, so near to me, lost that rich and beautiful earthly life, how will it be with you? She disobeyed a direct command.[33]

A few weeks later in September 1902, when he asked who

would join his Restoration Host - formed out of the disbanded Zion Seventies - unsurprisingly there were few dissenters. Four thousand people stood to their feet and repeated the Restoration Vow,

> I recognise John Alexander Dowie, General Overseer of the Christian Catholic Church of which I am a member, in his threefold prophetic office as the Messenger of the Covenant, the Prophet foretold by Moses and Elijah the Restorer. I promise to the fullest extent of all my powers, to obey all rightful orders issued by him directly or by his properly appointed officers and to proceed to any part of the world, wherever he shall direct as a member of Zion Restoration Host and that all family ties and obligations and all relations to all human government shall be held subordinate to this Vow, this Declaration and this Promise. This I make in the presence of God and of all the visible and invisible witnesses.[34]

The Restoration Vow was a highly questionable commitment for anyone to make, far less a Christian whose highest calling is surely to Christ.

When criticised, Dowie argued he only asked people to follow him in as far as he followed Christ. Even if that were true, given Dowie's interpretation of scripture was the only one that mattered, it is hard to see where that line now fell.

According to Dowie, since the Bible was not always clear, God had appointed him as the interpreter about latter-day matters.[35]

THE 'APOSTATE' METHODISTS

In the strange but inevitable way God has of bringing everything in darkness into the light, the visit of James Monroe Buckley editor of the Methodist Episcopalian *Christian World* would sound the death knell over Dowie.

Buckley was a long-standing opponent of divine healing. He thought it was no more than the inner healing power of the human body, whereby sufferers recovered by connecting with the "latent viral force" in their constitution.[36]

Dowie was no stranger to Buckley's views and wrote to the *Christian Colonist* as far back as 1886 - "Men like Dr Buckley are ready to admit every explanation for phenomena, except that of divine intervention."[37]

Perhaps in his new role as Elijah, Dowie relished the opportunity to put "men like Buckley" in their place. Or maybe, as Lindsay believed, Dowie looked for some sign that the other denominations were coming round to his way of thinking.[38]

Whatever his motivation, when the local Chicago Methodist Bishop asked to meet and bring Buckley along, Dowie readily agreed.

On the surface, the meeting was polite and restrained. Dowie stood unshakable in his conviction that divine healing was from God and in his self-belief as Elijah. Buckley played the long game and let Dowie hold centre stage.

So much so, Dowie thought the meeting went in his favour and released Buckley from his vow that their discussions would remain private. He agreed that Buckley could write an introduction to an article on Zion by a young reporter for *Century* magazine.

Buckley showed his true colours when the October 1902 edition of *Century* printed his no-holds-barred exposition of Dowie's -"consuming ambition, insatiable love of power, intense self-consciousness, grasp on money and property, vigorous suppression of individuality, commercialism, luxurious way of living."[39]

He contrasted this with John the Baptist and with Elijah and concluded,

> Reason must first be paralysed, faith drugged and this done, it would still seem too large and abnormal a conception for open-mouth credulity to believe that the Christ of the New Testament should choose the evolver and centre of such a flamboyant mixture of flesh and spirit to be the Restorer and his special forerunner. If Dowie believes it, he is in the moonlit borderland of insanity where large movements of limited duration have sometimes originated. If he believes it not, he is but another imposter.[40]

Annoyance at the scathing write-up would have been understandable. Dowie could have written a rebuttal. He could have pointed out that Buckley had no scientific proof for his hypothetical 'latent viral force' to explain away divine healing. He could have highlighted the numbers of Zion converts and the multiple testimonies of divine healing throughout his ministry.

But Dowie was not known for his "moderation to all men" or

indeed to any men. Rage engulfed him. How dare Buckley write such slander! He began to rally his army to give Buckley a "spanking."[41]

The Restoration Host would conquer Buckley on his own ground, New York.

THE ARMY GETS MOBILISED

Dowie went into overdrive with the New York mission. Maps were diligently studied, and the ethnic mix the city analysed in preparation for a house-to-house mobilisation covering the entire city. Thousands of dollars were splashed out on new uniforms, silk hats and frock coats for leaders.[42]

The Zion City Band prepare to leave for New York

Unfortunately by this time money flowed out of Zion Bank, a lot quicker than it flowed in. The timing of the crusade could not have been worse. Zion was still in a state of development and every dollar needed to support the growth of the community.

Excavations for the much anticipated Temple began shortly after the Third Feast of Tabernacles in July 1903, with a $5,000 steam shovel purchased to start the work.[43]   Amid much celebration, Dowie took out the first few shovels of dirt and a special collection raised enough money for "two perhaps three shovels."[44]

But after only five weeks, the first shovel disappeared, repossessed for non-payment.[45]   No one knew where the collection money went and no one liked to ask.[46] The hole in the ground, matched with the hole in Zion Bank where it was last seen.

Perhaps by more than coincidence, Zion land mortgages were due for payment a few weeks later in September 1903. Dowie deferred payment and paid interest only, confidently expecting to return from New York several million dollars richer.[47]

NEW YORK, NEW YORK

Participation in the mission became "practically a test of loyalty of a resident of Zion."[48]   Dowie grandiosely announced, "The Restoration Host is under vow as a standing army of peace to go wherever I, as Elijah the Restorer, may order it to go, at any time and under any condition."[49]

By this time the outside world tended to treat Dowie with a varying degree of scepticism and almost a grudging respect. They knew he could raise huge sums of money and commanded the loyalty of thousands of people. But he just seemed so outlandish. What do you say about someone who calls himself Elijah, yet travels first-class and can command an army?

The New York press publicised the mission, but without the same animosity of some of the Chicago newspapers. They were prepared to wait and see how it all worked out for Elijah II.

On 17 October, eight chartered trains took the Restoration Host to New York. On the following day, fourteen thousand people crowded into Madison Square Garden to be greeted by an impressive display of photographs of Zion City, with supporting materials from Zion Industries and Zion Land and Investment Association.[50]

Dowie at Madison Square

The days of the Little Wooden Hut must have seemed like a distant memory at the sight of the great Dowie, flanked by his adoring followers. An impeccably dressed five-hundred strong choir marched in, accompanied by the Zion Band and followed by the Restoration Host.

The atmosphere was electric as Dowie stood to his feet to deliver a crushing blow to the Buckleys of the world.

If Dowie had achieved in New York, what he did in the old days of Zion Tabernacle, the scoffers would have been silenced, and the sceptics left scratching around for explanations of the impossible become possible.

It didn't happen. The mission, conceived in anger and funded with Zion's badly-needed money, flopped. Dowie went there to settle a personal score with Buckley and, amid the songs, the marching and the smart new uniforms, "He wist not that the Lord was departed from him." (Judges 16:20).

When he stood to speak, in a pre-planned tactic, groups of people began to noisily leave the hall.[51] Dowie's confusion led to ranting and incoherent rage. "Bar the doors!" he screamed. But his words cut little ice with the brash New Yorkers. They came to see the great Dowie in action. They wanted a show. They got one – but more in the realm of a flailing gladiator than the prophet Elijah.

The Restoration Host looked on powerless to assist their leader, while reporters at the press desks busily penned copy for the next day's newspapers. He turned his anger on them, screaming insults. They were "dogs," "curs," "dirty yellow dogs," and "dirty, hungry dogs."[52] The abuse kept flowing, and they kept scribbling. One New York editor counted at least eleven variations of the word "dog" from a total of thirty-five insults![53]

Dowie's actions appalled those who would have given him an objective hearing and delighted those who came to bait him. In his better days, he could have turned the whole thing around, but he went into spiritual warfare in New York wielding weapons of the flesh, not weapons of the Spirit.

One commentator wrote, "Dowie's buffoonery, a horrible travesty of his religious profession, did not 'go' here for New York can laugh any fool off the stage."[54] He was kinder in his assessment of Dowie's followers,

> In proportion as New York was disgusted by the antics and pretensions and extravagance of the Prophet, so she was impressed and edified and amazed by the decency and orderliness and piety of his devoted Host. Such a contrast between a spiritual shepherd and his flock is rarely seen, and I for one am convinced that the real Dowie was not disclosed at the Garden performance.[55]

Would the real Dowie ever be seen again? The man who once sold his furniture to pay for evangelistic services seemed to be gone forever.

REPUDIATES HIS FATHER

He banned most of the newspapers from covering the services and then proceeded to argue with them over how many people turned up. [56] According to Dowie, it was seventy thousand. The *New York Sun* reported these figures as "Elijah's Delusions" and said Madison Square Garden had only eight thousand seats.[57] The *True Republican* put attendees at fifty thousand when it reported on "Riotous Scenes."[58]

Whatever the numbers were, Dowie made his mark but not for the best of reasons. Jeanie Dowie departed for Australia before the end of the mission with Gladstone.[59] The crusade then sank to a new low when the *New York World* published an angry letter from Dowie to his father.

184

John Murray Dowie had joined his son in Zion after his wife died in Australia.[60] After a glowing initial welcome,[61] things turned sour between father and son. John Murray was uncomfortable with his son's prophetic revelations, and Dowie cut him off without a penny for being a trouble maker.

Dowie's letter read that John Murray's "senile folly" was "utterly loathsome" to him. He blasted his father as a fool to write a "Dear son" letter and ask for his $125 a quarter allowance. The tirade went on,

> The kind-hearted woman whose love you so deeply abused for so many long months before you married her has gone to her God, and I trust in his love and mercy for my poor mother's eternal future. But as for looking upon you as a 'father' the thing is too utterly horrible to contemplate without anger and disgust.[62]

It was unclear how the newspaper obtained the letter and Dowie may have been correct in his assumption his father was behind it.[63] But his subsequent actions were entirely disproportionate, if not bizarre in the extreme. He launched a furious tirade at the press and told the five thousand people gathered; his birth father was a mystery romantic figure who died in the Crimean War.[64] He was of Royal blood and his mother forced by her family to marry a man she didn't love.

The hankies came out in Madison Square Garden, as the faithful dabbed their eyes at this fanciful story of a poor young girl wronged. Dowie omitted to tell them his mother was a thirty-three-year-old widow by the time she married her apprentice and tenant, twenty-year-old John Murray Dowie.

The young man who walked up to Edinburgh's High Street in 1854 with his son's hand in his, was now an old man, alone in a foreign country. An old man who looked so much like his son that people often mixed them up.[65]

For over fifty years, he tried to do the best for his son. Brought him up in a Christian home. Paid for his education in Edinburgh.[66] Used his connections to obtain Dowie's first posting in the Congregational church.[67] Bought him the clothes he preached in when he left the Congregational Church.[68] Now that same son stood before thousands of strangers and repudiated him as a fraud and a deceiver.

The news went round the world, within hours across the oceans to Australia where his family and friends still lived.

John Murray's humiliation was complete. The newspapers went looking for him, and he told them,

> The statement that I am not the father of John Alexander Dowie is the greatest myth ever uttered by the mouth of man. It is scandalous that my son should repudiate me after I have done so much for him. He is my son and born in lawful wedlock. No one can deny it. The record may be had at the General Register Office, Princess (sic) Street Edinburgh. I have always lived a quiet, peaceful Christian life and it breaks my heart to have this trouble come toward the end.[69]

Though devastated at his son's betrayal, John Murray maintained Dowie's mind was confused. He was "a poor soul," and still his son, whether he repudiated him or not.[70]

186

The New York trip cost $300,000, a whole year to plan, and a few short days to fail so miserably. Dowie put a positive spin on the mission. They evangelised the entire city. Three saloons had closed, and eighty baptisms took place.

But only a hundred and twenty-five new members were added to the church[71], and Dowie returned to Zion with his pockets empty.

14 THE WOLF AT THE DOOR

**Dowie with Deacons
Wilhite and Lewis**

"Dowie is the healthiest bankrupt I've ever seen."
Federal Custodian Paul Redieski

AT THE BEGINNING OF December 1903, Dowie's creditors made an application to the courts to declare him bankrupt.

If Dowie was bankrupt, so too was Zion and nearly everyone in it. They would lose their homes, livelihoods, savings and any money they borrowed to give to Dowie.[1] Despite his claims to outstanding business acumen, Dowie had performed extremely poorly at keeping Zion afloat. The investors got their dividends out of new investments, not profits, which meant he needed a constant supply of money coming in just to keep Zion afloat.

CRASH AT ZION CITY

Dowie's Property All in Hands of Federal Court

RECEIVERS APPOINTED

Rock Island Argus,
2 December 1903

His vision was of a Heavenly Kingdom, not an earthly one and Zion City, a means of funding his plans and projects. For others, it was their life and livelihood. How they put bread on their tables. How they bought fuel for their fires to see them through the cold Chicago winters. Their homes were built on land that did not belong to them, or indeed to Dowie. The mortgage holders still hadn't got their money, and $215,000 was due for payment.[2]

No one thought at the Watchnight Service in 1899 it would come to this. Where was all the money that could be made?

The huge profits expected from selling developed land were a fantasy. Dowie didn't want the world in Zion City – he only wanted his followers. To make matters worse, most of them were dependent on the city for their living. Twenty-five percent of the population didn't work and relied on their share dividends for income.[3] But the factories, starved of capital input, could neither pay the wages of the workers nor buy raw materials to make stock and generate profit.

There was still some wealth in Zion, but there was also

extreme poverty. Many of Dowie's followers lived in poorly constructed wooden houses and could scarcely afford to feed themselves, far less bail out Dowie.

In customary attack mode, Dowie refused to recognise any problems with his leadership and instead blamed "Masonic craft" for the financial troubles. [4] Zion was sound he told his followers, as he quoted the *Chicago Inter Ocean* to say how ludicrous it was that a creditor with an outstanding debt of $1,169, put a city worth ten million dollars into bankruptcy![5]

But the initial summons led to a raft of other creditors, also looking for their money. The total debt claimed amounted to a reported $385,000.[6] With the bankruptcy suit filed, things were now in the hands of the courts.

Fortuitously for Dowie, the judge in charge of the case was the older brother of his acquaintance Herman Kohlsaat. And mindful that many were in danger of losing their homes and livelihoods, Judge Kohlsaat issued an order forbidding bankruptcy and put the city into receivership until the accounts could be examined.

LOCKDOWN

Things looked grim for Zion. The city went into lockdown with the Zion Guard patrolling the outskirts on ponies to keep outsiders at bay.[7] Zion Bank closed its doors, guarded by United States deputy marshals.

The accounts showed Dowie as "the healthiest bankrupt" Federal Custodian Redieski said he had ever seen.[8] Yet inexplicably, there was only $12,000 in the bank.[9] Three dollars per head with a population of four thousand and hardly enough to cover one week's wage bill.

Where had all the money gone? That was the big question, but the immediate problem facing most people in Zion was keeping body and soul together without an income. Dowie said they would work for nothing, as long as they had food. Already since the failed New York trip, Zion workers received coupons instead of wages, which could be used as tithes or in Zion Stores.

But even that proved a problem since the receivers refused to authorise coupons guaranteed by Dowie, while he was under investigation for bankruptcy. Stores Manager Deacon Clendinen warned without using the vouchers, many in Zion would starve.[10]

On the following day, Judge Kohlsaat authorised the coupons, at the discretion of the receivers.[11] News went around like wildfire, and within hours, the shelves in Zion Store were cleared out.

THE COURT CUTS DOWIE A BREAK

With the future of so many people hanging in the balance, the court was loath to intervene. On 9 December 1903, they dissolved the receivership with the attorneys on both sides satisfied Dowie could pay his debts with some remedial measures put in place. Zion would pay the immediate debtors, and the others agreed to longer term payment terms.[12] Dowie would remain subject to the court until he paid off all the debts and pending that, the city would operate on a cash-only basis.

Helpfully, the landowners agreed to extend the debt on the

mortgages for a further year. They were worried a receivership would eat up any available funds and still had faith they could get their money with Dowie in charge.[13]

The moment of crisis was over and, having narrowly averted a disaster of catastrophic proportion, Dowie was unrepentant. He told Shiloh Tabernacle, "I am not going back an inch." Elijah the Tishbite had run away. John the Baptist did not follow Christ as closely as he should have. Dowie would outdo them both and stay his course.[14] Zion would stand firm on its principles.

And on that note on 1 January 1904, he left Deacon Speicher in charge and left for a world tour, "for the benefit of people of the whole world."[15]

Around the World Visitation Party

WORLD VISITATION

The World Visitation Tour showed how out of touch with reality Dowie had become. In one of his few caustic comments, Lindsay called much of the trip, "no more than a sight-seeing tour."[16]

It was an expensive one - fifty thousand dollars in total. The party travelled first class while leaving Zion labouring for coupons or "hot air money" as the vouchers became known.[17]

In February 1904, the Candy Factory closed temporarily and

the Furniture Store for good. The Candy Factory was a profitable business, but there was no money to buy supplies to produce stock.

In Dowie's absence, Speicher made some positive changes. Wages were cut across Zion - top officials by 50% and workers by 20%.[18] Unemployed Zion workers were also authorised to go to nearby Waukegan and seek employment to bring in some cash money.

Their leader was experiencing no such tightening of the belt. Accompanied by his party – most of them friends and family - he travelled through San Antonio and Los Angeles, on to Honolulu, New Zealand and then to Australia, where Wilbur Voliva, overseer of Zion in Australia met them.

Things did not go well in Australia. Dowie's attacks on King Edward riled up the patriotic Australians and riots broke out in Sydney, Adelaide and Melbourne.[19] He was forced to cancel evening services, and after visiting some of his old churches, the party moved on to Europe. By this time, trouble seemed to follow him wherever he went. Every hotel in London refused to take his booking and embarrassingly, the best he could do was to lodge with one of his church members, before persuading the Hotel Cecil to accept his party.[20]

In June, the Prophet of Restoration sailed for America and made his way back to Zion via Chicago, staying on the train throughout. Publicly he claimed he didn't want "to get the dirt of Chicago on his feet."[21]

Rumour had it the truth was more serious. 'Dr Dowie' the divine healer was ill.[22]

THE CONQUEROR RETURNS

The Zion inner circle now operated a conspiracy of silence with a constant stream of positive stories in *Leaves of Healing* muting any fears of the rank and file.[23]

Dowie arrived back to a hero's welcome with a triumphal fifty-foot arch built over Shiloh Boulevard. Each block bore the name of a city he had visited, with the names of those that shunned him painted in red.

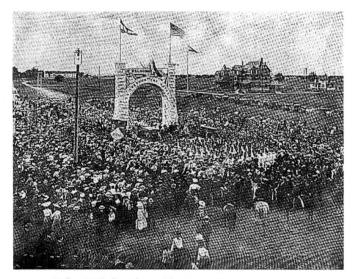

The Visitation Party returns

The Restoration Host marched to the station to meet their leader, accompanied by the Zion Band playing, "See the Conquering Hero Comes." Deacon Speicher eulogised that the coming of Elijah had once again brought rain, after an extended period of drought. The clouds converged on Zion from all directions as the presence of God went before his servant.[24]

Against such a backdrop, there seemed little to arrest Dowie's descent into 'madness.' Shortly after his return, he announced that he would invade London with a fleet of gospel ships in retaliation for the slight in barring him from the city's hotels. He asked Zion who would go and six thousand people dutifully stood to their feet.[25]

THE FIRST APOSTLE

Life in Zion was an unfolding drama. Just when it looked like it might all be over, the curtain came up again, and Dowie appeared centre-stage, reinvented as some new character from the Bible.

At the Fourth Feast of Tabernacles in July 1904, seventy nationalities in native dress marched around the *still* undeveloped Temple site. The festival was a celebration of the global vision of Zion and Dowie chose the occasion to announce "the Crown will be worn not only by us in Zion but by the many Zion cities which are to follow this."[26]

It was the run-up to the announcement of a vast site in Mexico that could be purchased for fifty cents an acre. The venture would silence those who walked around with "the mark of fear on their faces" - a shot aimed at Speicher, who was increasingly concerned about Zion's finances.[27]

Dowie mocked, "What splendid reformers you are! How large your spirit is! Oh, how magnificently you miserable creatures have understood the teachings of Zion and the mind of God!"[28]

As ever, Dowie was there to tell Zion "the mind of God" and on 18 September 1904, he had another fortuitously-timed prophetic revelation. Addressing Shiloh Tabernacle, he wore a long white satin garment, topped by a purple satin robe, fringed with gilt and embroidered with religious imagery. On his head sat a white silk turban with two purple bands.

He told the awestruck crowd, "Clothed by God with Apostolic and Prophetic authority, I now have the right to speak as the instructor of the nations."[29]

From then on, Dowie announced, he was to be known as *John Alexander, First Apostle,*[30] and in his role as the First Apostle, he would not be limited to the Bible. He was there to bring fresh revelation to the people of God.[31]

There was not "an atom of doubt" in his mind as to the Divine call to "this Office."[32] But exactly what that "office" was, seemed to have existed only in the First Apostle's mind. Dowie's "primitive order" had lost touch with anything hitherto known in Christian churches, both ancient and modern. It was a strange amalgamation of Jewish ritual, mixed with the gifts of the Spirit and eschatological expectations.

Escorted by a flag-bearing guard of honour, he announced that he would spend the next two weeks at his summer home Ben MacDhui in Michigan. His health was poor due to long vigils of prayer, his weight had decreased by twenty pounds, and he needed to rest.[33]

196

WE'VE CREATED A MONSTER

Zion had created its monster in Dowie, with its flag-waving and adoration. And through the authority of his new Apostolic Office, he made the rather worrying announcement,

> Since the Triune God has made us in the Triune image, no limitation can ever be placed upon the possible variety of Divine embodiments.[34]

There seemed little left to stand in the way of a new announcement that Dowie was perhaps the Incarnation after all! His leaders certainly feared the worst. There were hushed whispers about Dowie's statements on the person of Jesus which owed more to Greek myths of the gods' love affairs with mortals, than the Biblical witness.[35]

But Zion's leaders were also painfully aware the city was hamstrung with debt. If Dowie went under he might take them all with him, so they tried to tolerate him in his eccentricities and somehow contain them. That held good until the last of his grand designs pushed them, one by one, over the edge.

PARADISE PLANTATION

The expected announcement of others to join him in the reconstituted primitive 'Apostolic College' did not materialise. Instead, Dowie travelled to Mexico to look over land for his planned new venture *Plantation Paradise*.[36]

By this time he looked upon Zion Bank as "his own personal bank"[37] and any money in it, at his disposal. He needed half a million dollars for Paradise Plantation and ordered everyone resident in Zion to deposit funds if they hadn't already done so. He had "no use for them" and would expel them from Zion if they did not comply with the instruction.[38]

He then went wider and asked his worldwide followers to sell their houses, stores and farms and join him in Zion. Anyone with money in any bank except Zion Bank, should close the account immediately and transfer their money to Zion Bank.[39]

Returning to Zion, Dowie waxed lyrically of the spectacular opportunity in Mexico. They would grow cotton, sugar cane and rice and utilise local labour and converts from southern climates. Food grown on the Plantation would be shipped to Europe and New York by Zion steamers to build up the Zion brand.[40]

The above Warrants are issued in denominations of $20, $50, $100, $500, $1,000 and $5,000.

Dowie lost no time in promoting stock to secure funds for the immediate purchase of the land and appointed entrepreneur John A. Lewis as General Manager for the venture.

The First Apostle refused to listen to anyone who urged

caution. He alone wore the apostolic mantle, and he alone would make decisions in Zion's interests. He would broker no opposition because for him that was what destroyed his predecessor Edward Irving when he listened to "poor, foolish people who said they were prophets when they were not."[41]

SICKNESS STALKS ZION

With each passing day to live in a Theocracy felt less that God was in charge of their lives and more that they were at the mercy of Dowie's whims. The city was uneasy and the ideal community beginning to unravel.

Despite the Restoration Vow of absolute loyalty, the lifestyles of the leadership aristocracy in Zion, with its stark contrast to the ordinary people, was beginning to grate. Jeanie Dowie, never good with the cold Illinois winters, went for yet another extended holiday in Havana, suffering from 'nervous exhaustion.' Dowie later joined her there.[42]

In Dowie's absence, his personal attendant Carl Stein fell ill with pneumonia. A former Chicago police officer and saloonkeeper, Stern had turned his life around under Dowie's preaching and wanted to serve both God and Dowie with devotion all of his life.[43]

He was an immensely popular figure in Zion and ran the Police and Fire departments. When the cable came from Nassau instructing him to travel there so that Dowie could pray for him, Stern didn't hesitate. He took a train to Miami and was about to board a ship when he died.[44]

Abigail Speicher also died in early 1905. Deacon John

Speicher had seen so many miracles and now buried his wife.[45] If sin was to blame for sickness, why was this happening?

In February 1905, the hitherto loyal stalwart Charles Barnard tendered his resignation. Barnard claimed to be on good terms with Dowie. However, he told the *Chicago Tribune,* Dowie's request to mortgage a piece of land for $250,000 had led to friction between them.[46] Paradise Plantation was also part of that argument, but Barnard refused to go into detail on it.

He hoped Dowie would come round to his way of thinking but spoke of "the ultimate ruin of Zion community unless the present financial policy is changed."[47] According to Barnard, the entire city was drowning in debt,

> Leases are not worth the paper they are written on. The only thing the people have is the word of Dowie. The statement Zion is only $70,000 in debt is absurd. Its only sources of income are contributions and the Lace Factory.[48]

Dowie hit back and claimed his enemies fabricated the stories to jeopardise his Mexican plans. Poor health was likely to be behind Barnard's decision to leave.[49]

But Barnard was not the only one to leave Zion. Deacon Charles Westwood, Barnard's personal secretary, had already gone in the previous November.[50] Westwood told the press he handed in three resignations and they refused them all and sacked him. "In Zion, you cannot resign," he wearily told the *Tribune.*[51]

Factory manager Deacon William Hamilton also left, along

with Deacon Johnstone, manager of the Lumber Association.[52] Deacon Houch went from the bricklaying works. There were rumours the Lace Factory was in difficulty.[53]

Dowie was unfazed with the defections and remained intent on pushing forward with his plans for Mexico. Alexander Granger arrived to fill Barnard's position as head of Zion finances. Barnard was now labelled by Dowie as the sole source of Zion's problems and a traitor.[54]

No one rose to Barnard's defence, but then no one wanted the real state of Zion's finances made public. Newcomb later signed a confession to say he purposely misled Zion through *Leaves of Healing*. He wrote bitterly that, while the bills mounted up, "Dowie was touring the world, travelling in the most expensive way, taking the highest-priced suites at the finest hotels, entertaining lavishly at various places."[55]

He clearly had a good insight into the matter. As part of the leadership elite, he was with Dowie on the World Tour, enjoying the same first-class travel arrangements and staying in the same expensive hotels.

But he was young and naïve. Like so many others in Zion's leadership, he kept his head down and his mouth shut.

Finally, some welcome news came from the courts. On 12 July 1905, a full year and a half since the bankruptcy proceedings were first filed, the case was dismissed. No new cases were lodged, and $400,000 had been paid back with interest.[56]

This could have been a turning point. Dowie still had the support of many of his chief officers in Zion. But he was becoming more eccentric by the moment. By August 1905, he decreed his followers should have a baby every year and that no one could marry without his consent.[57] Zion had gone from a great pageant to a great parody of the gospel. Broke, in debt and getting weirder by the day. It could not continue. Something had to give.

WEIGHED IN THE BALANCE

Things were so different now from only a few years before when the first pilgrims visited the shores of Lake Michigan and saw the land that would become Zion City.

That day when they marched around the Temple site, waving their flags and proclaiming the Times of Restoration had come. That day when Dowie shouted out to them,

> Are you willing to obey God?
> Voices - Yes.
> General Overseer - Are you willing to come into a city where God rules?
> Voices - Yes.
> General Overseer - Are you willing to come into a city where God rules by me?
> Voices - Yes.
> General Overseer - I love you. I will give my life for you, but I will not let you rule me. Is that right?
> Voices - Yes.
> General Overseer - May God paralyse my tongue, lay low my right hand; may he cause my heart to cease to beat before I break the vow which I now make which is written in his Word - "One that ruleth over men righteously that ruleth in the fear of God."[58]

God does not forget. He is gracious, kind and always acts to bless us. But there are times in our lives when he needs to hold us accountable for our actions, for our good and that of the people around us.

He held Dowie accountable, and it only took a moment for God to write his end on the wall of Shiloh Tabernacle. On 24 September 1905, at a regular Sunday service, Dowie took the platform, clothed in the ornate gowns of the First Apostle. The service went on five hours, and towards the close, Dowie changed into his white robes to serve communion.

Suddenly he seemed to stumble and shook his right hand "as though some foul thing clung to it."[59] He banged it on a chair but to no avail. The crowd looked on perplexed, as Dowie's aides rushed to his side and hurried him off the stage.

Dowie had suffered a stroke. His right hand was paralysed and never again would he lift his booming voice in Shiloh Tabernacle.[60] His heart kept beating for a season but his days were numbered.

Mene mene tekel upharsin.

15 THE ACCUSERS

Voliva reads the charges against Dowie

"Many bulls surround me,
strong bulls of Bashan encircle me."
Psalm 22:12

HE LEFT FOR MEXICO in the following week, in the hope that a change of climate would improve his health. A series of upbeat letters followed on how much better he felt and the numerous opportunities afforded by Paradise Plantation.[1]

By Thanksgiving, Dowie was back in Zion, to a rousing welcome from the Zion City Band. Despite the party atmosphere, one look at Dowie's face and it was evident to everyone, he was a gravely ill man.[2] A valiant attempt to preach in Shiloh Tabernacle left him breathless and weak, and he was forced to give up halfway through.

By the middle of December, Dowie could scarcely speak and breathed with difficulty. He slept only a few hours each night due to "great discomfort through poor circulation."

He mused it may be God's judgement for "too much centralisation in Zion,"[3] and left again for Jamaica, a week before Christmas.

THE TRIUMVIRATE

Barnes, Speicher and Granger were authorised to run Zion's affairs in his absence. The financial situation was at a critical point with two hundred thousand dollars still outstanding on Zion land.[4] Something had to be done and done quickly, to avert financial ruin. The landowners were on the brink of legal action.

The Triumvirate rose to the moment and announced an immediate reorganisation of Zion business practices. Dowie would confine himself to ministerial work, and the stockholders would elect a board of directors to run Zion industries.[5]

The changes would lead to a root and branch overhaul, with outside businesses permitted to operate in Zion.[6] The restructuring would be placed in the hands of Barnard, and the system of pooling resources into a common fund stopped, as this had proved ineffective.[7]

News coming out of Zion reassured the creditors, with the attorney for two mortgage holders, owed a total of $117,000, satisfied "a new day is dawning for Zion City." He advised his clients not to proceed with legal action against Dowie.[8]

Despite the widespread optimism, Dowie fumed at what he

saw as insubordination. He cabled Voliva, Overseer in Australia, gave him power of attorney and told him to return at once to Zion. In the meantime, Gladstone was despatched back to Zion to take control of affairs.[9]

In mid-January, a further telegram arrived for Speicher, suspending him for officiating at a wedding that Dowie had not approved and acting as "the Devil's matrimonial agent."[10] Speicher stepped down but continued as a key figure in the management of the city. Zion needed him, and he needed Zion. He knew Zion was teetering on the brink of ruin.

VOLIVA

Help was at hand when Voliva arrived on 12 February 1906. Although offered Shiloh House, he moved into Elijah hospice because he wanted to be "near the people."[11]

Voliva asked for sacrifice and assured everyone he would be the first in line. His support for Dowie was unquestionable, as long as Dowie was pure. But ominously he added, "One divine principle applies to everyone. Disease is the result of sin."[12]

How that sat with Speicher, who had recently lost his wife, was unclear. But Speicher couldn't do it alone. Dowie was still a powerful man, even at a distance.

By this time, Dowie had recovered enough to move to Mexico. In March, he cabled for more money for personal expenses. The $4,500 given to him out of the Mexico fund was gone, and he had borrowed a further $3,000 on the strength of more money arriving from Zion.[13] Granger authorised a lower sum and suggested Dowie curb his spending like everyone else in Zion.[14]

It was a red rag to a bull. Another furious telegram arrived, reminding Voliva his appointment was only temporary. Every officer who opposed the Paradise Plantation was to resign forthwith, including Granger.

Fearing more dismissals, the leaders called an urgent cabinet meeting to formulate a plan of action. The course they decided on was astounding and audacious, given their earlier devotion to Dowie. Voliva had power of attorney and would sell the entire estate to Granger at a nominal sum of one dollar. That would take Zion out of Dowie's hands and enable them to make the decisions required to rescue the city.[15]

With the agreement made, Voliva lost no time and went to Waukegan to file a warrant deed, transferring to Granger all the real estate held by Dowie in Zion City, horses, carriages, books and furniture.[16] Within twenty-four hours it was all over. Dowie had lost Zion.

SUSPENDED FROM OFFICE

The cabinet then despatched a telegram to Dowie, suspending him from the position of General Overseer.

Zion City, Illinois, 2 April 1906. Dowie, Ocotlan, Mexico.

> You are hereby suspended from office and membership for polygamous teaching and other grave charges. See letter. You must answer these satisfactorily to officers and people. Quietly retire. Further interference will precipitate complete exposure, rebellion, legal proceedings. Your statement of stupendously magnificent financial

outlook is extremely foolish in view of thousands suffering through your shameful mismanagement. Zion and creditors will be protected at all cost.

It was signed by Overseers Voliva, Piper, Brasefield, Excell, Speicher and Cantel.[17]

The rout was incredible, after years of hero worship of Dowie. Everybody expected changes, but the speed at which they happened was breath-taking. Was Dowie really finished? Voliva told the newspapers,

> I have acted in this matter under the power of attorney which I possess. What has been done, I believe will be for the good of the church in Zion City and for its creditors. Legal counsel has been retained, and everything was carried out in accordance with their advice. We shall go ahead and put the affairs of Zion City in good order. If further steps are taken, it will depend on what is done by Dowie. The situation is up to him as it stands.

Voliva promised a statement in his accusation on polygamous teachings. The teachings were not based on public teaching but were of "a private character."[18]

GLADSTONE AND JEANIE

The polygamy allegations filled the newspaper headlines over the days to follow, both in Chicago and across the world. But it never actually got bottomed out why these past allegations did not surface earlier.

Where was the righteous indignation of Zion's leaders when the statements were supposedly made?

There is a definite sense the charges were contrived to serve a purpose. That Dowie made declarations which were, at best, unwise seems clear. But that he seriously intended to conduct sexual relations in 1906 with seven younger women when he could scarcely breathe, stretches the imagination.

> # GRAVE CHARGES
> # AGAINST DOWIE
> ---
> ### Deposed Leader of Zion City Accused of Making Polyga-mous Overtures
> Pittsburg Press, 3 April 1906

Indeed many of the more lurid accusations against Dowie seemed to originate with Jeanie Dowie.[19] Whether she was a jealous woman who made his life a misery as claimed by Dowie,[20] or a neglected and disenfranchised wife is a moot point. Jeanie frequently spent long periods apart from Dowie, and their relationship hardly mirrored the public image they tried to portray.

Gladstone Dowie had a lot on his shoulders. His mother was on the verge of a breakdown, and he thought Voliva's telegram might kill his father. If that didn't happen, Dowie would rush home in a rage, and the journey would finish him off.[21]

He was as loyal to his father as any son could be, given the circumstances. Gladstone had lived a life of incredible privilege, albeit in his father's shadow, travelling the world, residing in the family's lavish homes.

Now Voliva told him there was no money in Zion Bank, no bread in the bakery, no supplies in Zion Stores. Men and women with hundreds of dollars owed to them, queued for hours to get a dollar or fifty cents. Thirty thousand dollars' worth of coupons couldn't be honoured, and people were literally on the brink of starvation.[22]

He sided with his mother and the other Zion leaders but argued the statements made regarding polygamy were the ramblings of Dowie's confused mind. He claimed to see his father experience bizarre delusions in Mexico, followed by periods of lucidity.[23]

Back in Mexico, Dowie raged at the 'betrayal' by his wife and his son, alongside the other 'traitors' in Zion. Voliva's power of attorney was revoked and given to Deacon Wilhite. All six Overseers were dismissed, and Dowie announced he was on his way back to Zion.[24] He clearly did not grasp the magnitude of what had happened. Wilhite's power of attorney was worthless since all Zion assets now belonged to Granger.[25] For his part, Granger ignored his dismissal and continued as financial manager of the city.

DOWIE'S WOES

The financial woes of Zion should have been enough. But to make doubly sure that Dowie would never again wield any power in Zion, a concerted effort was made to blacken his name.

On 6 April 1906, over two hundred and fifty Zion leaders gathered to hear the case against their leader. Jeanie spoke of the conduct of her husband in the last two years. He had planned a harem with seven wives. A young Swiss heiress, Ruth Hofer, was to be the first and he had proposed to five others. Paradise Plantation was to be a polygamous colony.[26]

Shock quickly turned to anger when the group learned Dowie outlined the plans to his Overseers on the week before he was stricken with paralysis. He wanted to divorce his wife on the grounds of incompatibility.[27]

Overseer George Mason compiled excerpts from Dowie's sermons to "prove" he was leading people down the road to polygamy.[28] Arthur Newcomb claimed Dowie had spoken of polygamous marriage since 1904, in connection with "the time of restoration of all things."[29] According to Newcomb, Dowie said adultery was forbidden, and that amounted to "a clear command for polygamous marriage."[30]

A search of Shiloh House revealed a secret bunker, hidden behind a heavily bolted iron door and furnished with a strange kind of bed. Pornography and wine bottles were also discovered.[31] Ruth Hofer lodged with a Mrs Ely, who told of cases of wine arriving from Miss Hofer's brother in Italy labelled *Italian Chianti from Vero Vinto*. According to Mrs Ely, Dowie and Miss Hofer surreptitiously drank the wine together in Miss Hofer's room.[32]

Most worryingly, amongst the general character assassination, Voliva claimed Dowie misappropriated a staggering two and a half million dollars from Zion funds.[33]

The accusations came in thick and fast - without Dowie there to defend himself. In the event, the secret bunker turned out to be on the advice of his Zion Guard, should his life be in danger.[34] The 'pornography' was a first edition copy of the historical novel *Gil Blas*,[35] the shame of which was less about the content and more the fact Dowie spent $600 of other people's money on it, while their children went hungry.

No evidence was produced that the suspect wine was fermented, other than that the inquisitive Mrs Ely had her "doubts."[36]

The weird looking bed was nothing more sinister than a weird looking bed. And as to the mysterious Miss Hofer, no evidence was presented to suggest their relationship was anything more than a passing infatuation on Dowie's part for a younger woman. Certainly, Miss Hofer seemed more interested in Gladstone than his father - a feeling the younger Dowie did not reciprocate.[37]

Dowie strongly argued his relationship with Miss Hofer was purely paternal interest, and the promised revelation of the "love letters" between the two showed nothing more than that.[38]

Although the loyal Judge Barnes argued any action against Dowie was preliminary, and no one could be condemned in their absence,[39] it was a foregone conclusion what the outcome of Dowie's trial in absentia would be. Zion's leaders abandoned him. With the leadership in Zion now firmly on his side, Voliva was confident he could go to the wider community.

VOLIVA TAKES THE STAGE

On 8 April 1906, a hush fell over a packed Shiloh Tabernacle as Voliva took the stage. Three thousand five hundred people waited to hear the case against their leader. All eyes were on Voliva as he stood, flanked by the co-accusers, holding up the evidence against Dowie.[40]

He launched into a virulent tirade against Dowie. He was a "spendthrift," "a liar," and "a traitor to the trust of his people."[41] Voliva told the crowd he was not like Dowie - he was like them.

Forced to keep his family of five on a salary of $50 per month, a tenth of which went to Dowie.

"What has become of all this money that has been flowing into Zion for so many years?" he asked. No one could say.[42]

When Speicher and Excell spoke of the immorality of Dowie's teachings, "too shocking to say but touching on the parentage of Jesus," the crowd listened aghast.[43] One man jumped to his feet and exclaimed, "You are a liar! You are lying!" Speicher answered that he only spoke of the facts[44]

When the show was over, Voliva dramatically asked who should be their leader, and the people declared Voliva to be that man. The Zion Guard were sworn in to protect the new General Overseer, and all agreed to transfer their allegiance with only one dissenter.[45]

Ripples of shock hit Zion worldwide. In Australia, Overseer M'Cullagh read out a litany of complaints against Dowie. Overseer Voliva was "in the know" and had sent him the full detail. Of the three and a half million dollars invested in Zion, only a million had gone into stock. The rest had gone on horses, books and Dowie's "ladies."[46]

Australia rejected Dowie. Churches across the world followed suit and within days, "from London, Zurich, New York, Milwaukee and Boston" they abandoned Dowie and sided with Voliva.[47]

TELL IT NOT IN GATH

"Tell it not in Gath...lest the daughters of the Philistines rejoice,"

David warned the Israelites after Saul's death. The oversight in Zion had no such qualms. They were quite happy to tell anyone who would listen that everything was Dowie's fault and they were the ones to save the day.

Yet, with the exception of Voliva and the newly-arrived Granger, the majority of them had been complicit in covering up the financial sham Zion had become. Samuel Packard, keen to clear his name, maintained,

> I have no doubt that Zion City and its numerous industries would be in a thriving condition to-day with Dowie still in absolute control if the original plans had been adhered to… The original plans never contemplated any such thing. They never intended that Dowie should appropriate money for his own use.[48]

Dowie's behaviours were presented as an unforeseen aberration, rather than the depressingly predictable outcome of the very structures Zion's leaders had willingly built. Did Packard forget those days back in Judge Tuley's courtroom when the little Samuel Stevenson stood in the dock, facing up to the sharp Chicago attorney? Did he forget that highly unusual contract he drew up and gave to Stevenson to sign? Did he forget that night in Central Tabernacle when Dowie trooped Stevenson's brothers on stage to denounce their own brother as a liar?

He was a top league lawyer, and it is not credible he didn't have at least a suspicion of what was going on. Packard's error was repeated across Zion. He counted Dowie as a god when he was but a man.

All eyes were now on Dowie to see what the fallen hero would do. The world's press knew Elijah II of old, and they thought he might have some life in him yet.

But it was all over, bar the humiliation. Keenly feeling the slights from his wife and son, Dowie hit back and said far from acting honestly, Jeanie and Gladstone had hoped to kill him with their behaviours. They were angry that he was not leaving them as much in his will as they thought they were due.[49] Jeanie Dowie had made his life a misery.[50] As for the stories that he gambled on Wall Street, that he had found the "law of Moses," or found ten million dollars in Mexico, they were all lies.[51]

Despite Dowie's denials, there appeared to be some semblance of truth to some of these reports. Gladstone Dowie said the ten million dollars was a hallucination Dowie experienced in Mexico.[52] And the accusation that Dowie lost $1.5 million on the New York stock exchange [53] would at least have accounted for where some of Zion's missing money went.

Jeanie was distraught. She changed allegiance and now maintained she would stand by her husband.[54] Dowie was unimpressed at the remorse. When he arrived at St Louis on route to Zion, he attacked her publicly saying he would not share his bed with "a dirty dog" and "a male demagogue."[55]

Gladstone hit back implying his father had an affair in 1877, a detail doubtless passed on from his mother, courtesy of the old Newtown gossips.[56] Dowie responded by attacking Gladstone as an "unnatural son."[57]

It was all descending into a farce. Old John Murray Dowie stoically stood by his son. He maintained Dowie's troubles came about because he was over-worked and his mind unbalanced.[58] These were mistakes made "in the greed for power forgetting that what God in his goodness has given him, that he can also take away."[59]

John Murray thought when Dowie came to his senses, he would resume his old place as Zion's leader. His generosity did not extend to poor beleaguered Gladstone, who his grandfather claimed had gone to three universities and would "never amount to anything."[60]

DOWIE ARRIVES BACK

Dowie arrived back in Chicago on 13 April to be met by a two thousand strong crowd, booing and jostling him. Gone were the days of the Triumphal Arch and the rapturous welcome of the Zion Band. Voliva went full throttle on the 'madness' of Dowie, but Dr Speicher, perhaps in a moment of regret when he saw the miserable condition of his old friend, said that Dowie was a very sick man and suffering from pulmonary troubles, paralysis and dropsy with sessions of delirium.[61]

Zion was not so much at war as in shock. Shock that their money was gone. Shock that their leader was shown to be less than the demi-god they supposed him. Shock that the dream of a Heavenly city had gone so horribly wrong. Anger and offence mingled with the hurt they felt. How could this happen?

At the suggestion of Judge Barnes, Dowie was allowed to live in Shiloh House. He moved in at the end of April [62] and obtained a court injunction to speak in Shiloh Tabernacle on alternate days.[63]

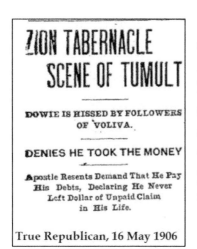

ZION TABERNACLE SCENE OF TUMULT

DOWIE IS HISSED BY FOLLOWERS OF 'VOLIVA.

DENIES HE TOOK THE MONEY

Apostle Resents Demand That He Pay His Debts, Declaring He Never Left Dollar of Unpaid Claim in His Life.

True Republican, 16 May 1906

A temporary thaw in relations saw Jeanie appear with him at Zion Tabernacle on 30 April. Dowie wore his robes but was supported by two attendants and delivered his message seated. Only a few of the old faithful were present, and the meeting turned into a brawl.[64]

Dowie's church was now that of "the coloured people."[65] White Zion had abandoned him. Most of them were listening to Voliva at a rival service held in Zion College. Voliva told them if Dowie was not insane, the word must be criminal.[66]

ZION BROKE

Dowie's lawyer petitioned the courts to rule that Voliva's power of attorney was invalid, as he overstepped his authority. He initially argued all of Zion's property belonged to Dowie personally, but then conceded 95% belonged to Zion and 5% should go to Dowie, approximately one million dollars.[67]

The attorneys were not able to reach an agreement, and Judge Kenesaw Landis heard the case over two weeks of bitter legal dispute. The scale of the alleged corruption was staggering. E.E. Hardwood teller of Zion City Bank gave evidence that Dowie was personally overdrawn by over $481,000."[68] On top of that, Zion Industries had combined overdrafts of $657,000.[69] Zion Bank had deposits of half a million dollars but hardly a dollar to pay out.

The Lace Factory had a paid up stock of $2.8 million and an actual investment of only $415,000. The operating loss was $1.2 million. The Candy Factory had a paid up stock of $155,000 but an actual investment of only $18,000, with a total operating loss of $93,000. In the supply manufacturing side, there was a paid up stock of $257,000 but an actual investment of only $22,000 and an operating loss of $249,000.

The rest of the industries told a similar story. Food supplies had a loss of $27,000; railway construction, a loss of $4,000; the printing house, a loss of $450,000; the hotel, a loss of $175,000; and transportation a loss of $11,000. A staggering $2 million had been diverted out of Zion, while losses of over $2.5 million were concurrently accumulated.[70]

These numbers mask the misery that stood behind them. They represented life savings, investments, hopes and dreams. It was a shocking tale of a community badly let down by both Dowie and by their leaders who stood by silent, afraid to incur the wrath of their leader.

DOWIE TAKES THE STAND

When Dowie took the stand, Voliva's lawyer attempted to prove his insanity by asking him to retell his spiritual visions. Dowie spoke of his vision of a golden city, first seen in Edinburgh when he was a young man.[71]

"Have you had any other visions?" asked Attorney Newman.

Dowie went on to tell of a "peculiar blue light" that burst into a thousand tongues of fire. All the while, beautiful music played all around him. On another occasion, he was warned to leave the church as an attempt would be made on his life. And on yet another, through prayer, God saved a ship he was travelling on.

Newman asked Dowie if, in assuming the role of Elijah the Restorer, he changed his personality.

Dowie replied, "I am still the same John Alexander Dowie who was born in Edinburgh in 1847, but some change must have happened in order that I might do the work mapped out for me."[72]

His nurse, Elizabeth McLennan, lodged an affidavit of delusional behaviours in Mexico when Dowie imagined the Emperor and Empress of Germany were coming to visit him.[73] John Murray Dowie testified that Dowie's soldier father was a figment of his son's imagination.[74] No mysterious soldier father died in the charge of the Light Brigade.

The Chicago press was always better with Dowie when he was on the offensive. They could understand an insult, but Heavenly visions were beyond their ken. They sided with Voliva and agreed that Dowie was mad.

Judge Landis wisely steered clear of ruling on spiritual experiences and confined himself to the legal argument. On 27 July 1906, he decided Zion property had been built up through contributions given to Dowie in his representative capacity, and as such, it was a trust estate. He ruled it should pass to Dowie's successor in the office of General Overseer.

Landis was unimpressed with Voliva and the other leaders' behaviours towards their former leader which he said exceeded their legal mandate.

Granger's power of attorney was revoked as he had taken the Restoration Vow. This outraged the patriotic Landis, who saw it as tantamount to "an obligation of dishonesty." He observed that while it was beyond his remit to express contempt for anyone who could take the Vow (thereby making his opinion more than clear), equally he was not obliged to put trust in a man who pledged to go against his family and country.

Dowie was given permission to remain in Shiloh House and Landis appointed a receiver, responsible for all Zion money and property until an election could be held for the position of General Overseer [75]

Dowie didn't put his name forward and on 18 September 1906, Voliva won the election.

16 LAST DAYS

"When they get ready for a better religion, they will moult Dowie, as the bird sheds its feathers when it begins to grow a better plumage."
Elbert Hubbard

THEY DID MOULT HIM as Hubbard predicted. The new regime painted over Dowie's name on the boards in Zion and ownership passed to Voliva. Within a short time, the leaders went their separate ways, with Voliva left holding almost as much power as Dowie once did – with more business acumen but significantly less anointing.

On the face of it, he started off well-intentioned, claiming he would "build factories for the workingmen and go down and work with them." He would, "absolutely do away with the aristocratic circle that has grown up in Zion."[1] As is the way of these things, it didn't quite happen like that. Once he drove everyone else out who didn't agree with him, Voliva proved even more dictatorial than Dowie.[2]

Did Dowie's followers move to a better religion? For many, the answer was yes. Voliva had no time for the gifts of the Holy Spirit. He thought dreams and visions were the work of the Devil.[3] He drove the Pentecostal faction out of Zion and the gifts of the Spirit with them.[4] They were scattered from Zion and went on to build the worldwide Pentecostal movement.

Dowie was left virtually penniless and alone. He continued to strenuously deny the allegations that he promoted polygamy and claimed to ask Voliva on several occasions for the proof. It was not forthcoming.[5] Although he wanted to leave for Mexico, in September 1906 those plans were cancelled at the last minute.[6] A vision had told him to stay and fight for Zion.[7] It was never going to happen. Dowie's last days were upon him.

The reconciliation to Jeanie proved short-lived.[8] The courts awarded her the summer home Ben MacDhui and Gladstone and John Murray Dowie joined her there.[9] Gladstone mellowed somewhat when he said his father was sincere, but that he possessed "a strange ability to be deceived."[10] Although he didn't reconcile with his father, Gladstone went on to become an Episcopalian minister.[11]

Dowie spent his last months in Shiloh House, with only a few friends as companions. Some of the old faithful remained, and

Dowie would address them on a Sunday morning in Shiloh House. But for the most part, Zion got on with its business.

In the closing months of his life, Dowie had time to reflect on his life - as Lindsay put it, "his triumphs and his tragedies." He had suffered abuse, poverty, even physical violence and came through it triumphantly. But there are few trials in life more deadly than the pride of our own heart.

Though his mind was confused at times due to illness, Dowie certainly wasn't mad. The dream was over, with only a lingering shadow of the anointing. Lindsay related that Dowie borrowed fifty dollars from one of his last remaining friends. The old man could scarcely afford to give the money, as he needed it for his mortgage. The next week to his amazement, his entire mortgage was paid off.[12] Judge Barnes proved a faithful friend and reconciled to Dowie in the last weeks of his life. Barnes tried unsuccessfully to heal the rift between Zion and Dowie, but Voliva denied his request to put an article into *Leaves of Healing*.[13]

ICHABOD

The newspapers missed Dowie. Zion's new regime wasn't half as newsworthy, or as entertaining, as Dowie in the old days. Voliva proved a stern and autocratic leader but without the Dowie charisma. The *Rockford Daily Register* reported in December 1906, "No quack or charlatan or mere pretender could accomplish the results that Dowie accomplished."

But sadly, they told their readers, "The end has come. Elijah has gone forever. There is no one to receive his mantle and a double portion of his spirit. Instead of the horse and chariots of

Israel, there is encamped a host of creditors...over the door is the handwriting on the wall 'Ichabod.' Its glory has departed."[14]

Chicago missed Dowie. For a good long while, he was the talk of the town and the breakfast table. But life goes on, and they found other things to talk about. God remembered Dowie. He didn't heal him, and despite Dowie's prayers, he didn't restore him. But he remembered him. Marie Burgess met a young cripple outside of Zion Stores where she worked. He was on his way to the rail station and told her, "I came here all the way from Australia because I wanted Dr Dowie to pray for me. I know if he would have prayed for me, I would have been healed."[15]

Marie's heart went out to the young man, and she found some willing helpers to carry the visitor in his wheelchair up to Dowie's bedside. Dowie was so weakened, he needed assistance to lift his paralysed hands and place them on the young man's head. In his frail failing voice, he uttered the words spoken over so many others around the world,

> In the name of our Lord Jesus Christ, by the power of the Holy Spirit and in accordance with the will of God, our Heavenly Father, let this man be free from every infirmity.

When they lifted Dowie's hands from the young man's head, he was healed. God had shown Dowie one last time, "He is risen with healing in his wings."

Dowie did not die at the hands of his enemies but of his Friend. On 9 March 1907, as the dawn broke over Zion, the Little White Dove carried Dowie into the presence of the Lord. Judge Barnes and his two personal assistants were with him.

"Long hath the night of sorrow reigned
The dawn shall bring us light
God shall appear, and we shall rise
With gladness in His sight."

"The Christ was there, and I rose with gladness."

John Alexander Dowie 1847-1907

"By the grace of God, a helper of men."

EPILOGUE

"How the mighty have fallen in battle!"
2 Samuel 1:25

IT IS HUMAN NATURE to remember the falling, more than the flying. David knew that which is why he reminded people to celebrate Saul's success and not glory in his downfall.

In that spirit, let's not leave Dowie at his point of failure. He began as a helper of men until his simple devotion to the gifts of the Spirit was buried amidst a torrent of bloated egotism and pride. Yet Dowie's legacy is immense. He raised the bar for the church as it moved into the last of the Last Days. His global ministry drew in adherents from all denominations, foreshadowing the twentieth-century charismatic movement.

He forged a spiritual dynamic that paved the way for the reception of the gifts of the Holy Spirit in the early Pentecostal movement. And he flew in the face of respectable Protestantism when he disputed the supposed division between the secular and the religious,

> ...everything that comes from God's Hand is something to be used in alleviating human misery, in increasing human knowledge, in removing human burdens, in leading humanity to him who forgiveth all their iniquities, healeth all their diseases and beareth all their burdens.[1]

Money was admittedly a huge failing for Dowie. He was a

poor steward, a trait built up over many years. But his inability to manage money does not negate the principles he stood for.

Dowie believed a poor church could never do the work of reaching the nations with the gospel. He sought to raise the living standards of the people of Zion and offer them a fair rate on their investments. A friend to the poor, rather than a pious philanthropist, he understood the structural inequalities that engender poverty. He wanted to build a society that would have God at its centre because "where God rules, man prospers."

This was no empty "prosperity gospel" but a far-reaching plan to create wealth and fund world mission. The programme for change went far wider than industry and finance. Dowie was a pacifist who believed in equality across race and gender. He recognised all forms of oppression are ultimately from the enemy.

One man was asked why he didn't abandon Dowie when he had to queue for fifty cents to buy bread and Dowie owed him hundreds of dollars. He told his story. Dowie's preaching led him to salvation when he lived on the streets of Chicago, a slave to drink and penniless. He came to Zion to dig ditches, got a job in the Lace Factory, and then became head of his department in *Leaves of Healing*. He stood by Dowie, despite his failings because, as he put it, "I will not lightly cast away someone who has done so much for me."[2]

He was only one of the countless numbers whose lives were transformed through Dowie's ministry. It is only speculation to imagine what Dowie could have done, had he remained faithful to his calling. But what he did achieve went far beyond many of his contemporaries. He is remembered as the man who thought he was Elijah. But in his heydey, he was the man who brought the Kingdom of God into a dark place. His values outlived him and are now foundational to any modern society that strives to be just and fair.

MEDIA AND TECHNOLOGY

Dowie led the way in the use of technology to promote the gospel. From his early use of a mechanical timestamp for prayer requests to Zion Publications that took the gospel of divine healing to the world, he wanted the Kingdom of God to be demonstrably living and active, not hidden away in a church building.

He used the emerging technology available to him, and his sermons were heard throughout the world through his pioneering use of phonographs. He would not be "trammelled" by what had been done to date, but rather use whatever means he could to reach the multitudes.

Although he didn't live to see radio and television available commercially, when he first saw them demonstrated at the Chicago and Paris World Fairs, Dowie recognised their enormous potential to spread the gospel.[3] As Dowie put it,

> Principles are eternal; Modes of Operation change. We now have powers to do what they never could have thought of doing in the olden time. We can carry that Message to the people by the printing press and soon by the phonograph, and in a thousand ways. I believe that these are the days when the Hidings of God's Power are being brought forth in many ways. I will not be trammelled by any modes

or forms that would weaken power. Forms of Godliness that have no power are a curse. Into every form we must put the Power; the Power that does the work and reaches the people.[4]

All of this was with one purpose – to preach the gospel to the nations and prepare the way for the Second Coming of Christ. When faced with a dying, sterile church, Dowie reminded people that the Kingdom of God is living and active, advancing and majestic. His God was not small and impotent, cowed by the advance of secularism. Far from it - his God was for him and with him.

DOWIE'S INFLUENCE

Dowie wanted to build the Kingdom of God, but he forgot he was a part of that Kingdom, not the consummation of it. Others would pick up his mantle and build on the vision he planted in them.

Three of the original eight members of the Assemblies of God General Council - J. Roswell Flower, Cyrus Fockler and Daniel Opperman - all began their ministries associated with Dowie. Carl Brumback documenting the beginning of the Assemblies of God wrote,

> Critics made much capital out of some of the later phases of Dowie's work, but it is the testimony of all who knew him that he was, in the beginning, a man signally and genuinely used by God for some undoubted miracles. Some of his followers became the first Pentecostal leaders.[5]

Charles Parham was an important catalyst to that when he visited Zion in September 1906. Parham built a sizable following, including John Lake and his Healing Rooms associate former Zion Band leader F.F. Bosworth. Voliva forced Parham out of Zion, and his group were scattered across America and beyond with their Pentecostal message. John Lake built on work by existing Zion missionary Daniel Bryant in South Africa and the churches that came out of that, largely shaped the face of African Pentecostalism.

Other prominent Pentecostals who emerged from Dowie's Zion were Fred Vogler, evangelist, Home Missions Director and Assistant General Superintendent of the Assemblies of God; Marie Burgess Brown, pastor of the Glad Tidings Tabernacle in New York City; Frederick Arthur Graves, songwriter, evangelist and pastor; and evangelist Lemuel C. Hall.

Dowie's former Overseer William Piper went on to pastor the Chicago Stone Church and publish *The Latter Rain Evangel*, in print for more than thirty years. Piper hired Anna C. Reiff, former secretary to Dowie. Under her leadership, the magazine "circulated Pentecostal teaching and news to a wide and far-flung readership."[6]

Yet more figures from the early Pentecostal movement include Martha Wing Robinson, faith healer and teacher; Gordon Lindsay, author and founder of Christ for the Nations Institute; Raymond Richey, evangelist and faith healer and Lilian Yeoman, evangelist, teacher and writer.

Dowie's followers also infused A.J. Tomlinson's Church of God with their belief in divine healing.[7] It became the second largest Pentecostal church behind the Assemblies of God.

Margaret Fielden, the daughter of one of Dowie's elders, married Harry Cantel, overseer for the United Kingdom. She left Zion with her husband to set up a Pentecostal group in London. When her husband died, Margaret continued to lead the work and ran a missionary guest house. Desmond Cartwright wrote, "the guest list became a veritable *Who's Who*."[8] And according to Donald Gee, it was "one of the best known and best beloved Pentecostal centres not only in London but the whole of the British Isles and far beyond."[9]

Healing evangelist Smith Wigglesworth began his healing ministry in Leeds, highly likely to be the Leeds outreach referred to glowingly in *Leaves of Healing*.[10] His wife Polly was baptised by Dowie on 13 October 1900, during Dowie's visit to London. Gerrit Polman, the father of Dutch Pentecostalism and a key figure in early European Pentecostalism, studied theology in Zion and became a Deacon before travelling back to Holland as a Dowie missionary.[11]

These are only some of the early Pentecostal leaders influenced by Dowie. The bigger story lies in the thousands throughout the nations who accepted the Pentecostal message of the gifts of the Holy Spirit through Dowie's teaching.

DOWIE AND DIVINE HEALING

For the vested interests of his enemies, Dowie was a fraud, while they hid behind a thin veneer of respectability. Elbert Hubbard saw through such deception as self-serving and shallow.

> The simple truth is, Dowie is a very much better man than any of these microbes who berate him…Dowie's weekly paper is a bouquet of violets compared with

any issue of any daily newspaper in Chicago. These papers with their details of woe, grime, crime, blood and death, to say nothing of personals and medical advertisements that no gentleman dare read aloud, all claim the privilege of referring to Dowie as a toilet room rodent.

Beware of the paper or person that mud-balls people. The epithet a man applies to another usually fits himself best. We describe that which we see. All the people who disparage Dowie you will find are in competition with Dowie.[12]

For some people today, Dowie is still a "toilet room rodent." But once you chip away at the veneer, underneath they are still in competition with him. By discrediting him, they believe they can discredit divine healing.

That will never happen because 'Dr Dowie' did his work and achieved his purpose in life. He brought a seismic shift in how a huge number of people in the church today view divine healing. God is not the author of sickness and can and frequently does, intervene through the medium of prayer and the gifts of the Holy Spirit.

As to Dowie's attitude to doctors, the medical profession is considerably wiser and more self-aware than it was in Dowie's day. Doctors are unlikely to prescribe addictive drugs, except as a last resort and surgical interventions are only done after informed patient consent. Doctors are clearly not "of the Devil," any more than any other profession. If they are limited by their knowledge, that doesn't make them evil. It makes them human. We can thank God for the tremendous strides made forward in medicine over the last hundred years that have saved millions of lives.

Dowie's views on proper sanitation as fundamental to well-being, have stood the test of time. His *auld enemy*, the Illinois Board of Health, remarked the hygiene and sanitation in Zion were "almost as sound from a sanitary standpoint as from a religious point of view." Their report concluded it would be a good thing for public health if other communities were as rigorous as Zion.[13]

Dowie didn't always get his theology right. Health is no measure of godliness when an atheist can be well, and a devout Christian lies sick. But his willingness to believe God to honour his Word through divine healing was outstanding, inspirational and world-changing.

WEAKNESSES

Previous biographers have looked for one trigger or crisis that torpedoed Dowie from his meteoric rise to fame and brought him low. The truth may be much simpler than that. Dowie believed in his principles; he just couldn't live up to them. His flesh let him down, and if he ultimately fell victim to the very evil he denounced, it only goes to show the truth of the scripture, "The love of money is the root of all evil" (1 Tim 6:10).

His anointing had dissipated in the last years of his ministry, but he was still held with enormous respect and affection by the people of Zion. As Judge Barnes put it in his address at Dowie's funeral, "There were times when the assembled thousands of Zion would have gone singing to the stake for John Alexander Dowie because they loved him."[14]

When it became known he had lived a double-life that devotion vanished overnight. People trusted him with their money. When they put money into Zion Bank and Zion industries, they had every right to expect it handled with godly stewardship. Instead, Dowie used it as his personal expense fund. That he used his spiritual gifting to raise that money made it tenfold worse.

Charisma is no guarantee of character and character isn't a one-off event. It is a lifestyle. But tell that to the woman whose blind child could see after Dowie's prayers. Tell that to the former cripple who could walk. These people can't be blamed for their unswerving devotion to Dowie. His closest associates should have spoken out sooner. They may not have realised the full extent of the financial mismanagement in Zion, but they knew enough. But in fairness, many of them were likewise psychologically beholden to Dowie, through the healing of a family member.

Was there a fear if they criticised Dowie, sickness would return? Yes - and there is also evidence Dowie encouraged that fear. Some years after Dowie's death, Alexander Boddy visited Zion and found people there who told him they were afraid to leave Zion in case their illness returned.[15] Such a level of spiritual abuse could not be allowed to continue. God stepped in and brought Dowie's reign to an end. That was the grace of God, not the judgment. And it speaks volumes for the practice of spiritual gifts in the church today and whether God can trust his people to be worthy stewards of them.

LEGACY

Zion City still stands today as a tangible reminder of John

Alexander Dowie's life and ministry. The factories are gone and the city governed in the same way as any other community. It is not quite as though he never lived. The streets still bear the Biblical names, but the songs of Zion have largely fallen silent.

It is either a sad coincidence or a divine providence that both Edward Irving and John Alexander Dowie had a revelation that history would not be kind to them. Irving wrote in the closing days of his life, "I discern that the Lord will utterly separate my name from the work which he worketh for the blessing of the whole world."[16]

Dowie echoed those words in 1899 when in Central Zion Tabernacle he wept and said,

> I sometimes fear that I shall be like Moses, having led this people on, I shall be set aside—yea God himself setting me aside and choosing another to lead the people on. I fear that I shall sometime say, Dowie did something when Dowie never did anything. I shall thus grieve God by taking some glory for myself when it all belongs to him.[17]

Those prophetic discernings proved right for both men. Only in recent years are they recognised as pioneers of the great moves of the Holy Spirit throughout the last century and only now are the links between the two men better understood.

Dowie's personal failure did not bring an end to what God was doing in the earth but rather the opening of a new chapter. Brian Stanley, Professor of World Christianity and Director of the Study of World Christianity at the University of Edinburgh, wrote,

236

He can be criticised for collapsing the biblical tension between the 'already' and the 'not yet', but he remained absolutely consistent in a country divided by racial antagonism to the principle that in the city of God there can be no distinction between black and white. Above all, for millions of Christians in the southern hemisphere today, his insistence that the salvation that Jesus came to impart is for the body as well as the soul and for this life as well as the life to come, is at the very heart of their faith.[18]

That is a fitting accolade to end on, and Edinburgh University can rightly be proud of Dowie. The young man who went back to *Auld Reeky* with an armful of books and a pocket full of dreams wanted to change the world. He did just that.

AUTHOR'S NOTE

I hope you've enjoyed reading about John Alexander Dowie. Please also do look at the Appendixes. 'God's Witnesses' brought Dowie's story alive to me and the illustrations by Charles Champe give a sense of what it was like to be part of the vision of Zion.

It was challenging to write about Dowie and lay him bare. It is easy to criticise, but few of us will have others pour over our life stories, long after we are dead. I guess there would be things in there most of us wouldn't want known. I've tried to be fair and balanced in telling Dowie's story, while immensely conscious this material may be disappointing to those who hold him in high regard. Dowie was an anointed man of God, yet still only a man. And as the saying goes, "The best of men are men at best."

Wherever possible, I used material written either by Dowie or by his contemporaries - although I did allow myself some poetic licence with Willie for the Prologue. Some time ago, I sat in Princes Street Gardens looking up at the Crags and thinking about Dowie. It kind of wrote itself in my head that day. Willie and Bessie were, however, historical figures from Dowie's life. And yes, he did beat Willie up for pulling Bessie's hair.

The rest of the material didn't write itself in my head and is based on verifiable sources, notably the stories of those healed. To paraphrase Dowie, these are not the stories of "Mr Nobody from Nowhere." They can be found in the yellowing copies of the stories of generations before us, who have now gone to glory, but whose testimony so profoundly affected our world today.

Gordon Lindsay's book on Dowie was also a great help, as was Philip Cook's detailed study of Zion. While some of Lindsay's material is unreferenced, as he had access to people who lived in Dowie's Zion, I felt it could be relied upon.

Lindsay tended to gloss over the less savoury aspects of Dowie's life. I understand the motivation behind that, and I have a lot of sympathy with his sentiments. But since Dowie is now gone for over a hundred years, I didn't feel too bad about telling the whole story, warts and all. Sometimes the parts we would want to omit are the key to understanding the whole picture.

If Dowie were to come back tomorrow – would he thank us for an edited version of his life, or would he rather ask us to learn from his mistakes? I think the latter. If life did not teach Dowie humility, then a hundred years in Heaven before the Throne of God will have more than rectified that deficit.

I was particularly sorry to dispel the belief, popularised by Lindsay and others, that Dowie literally prophesied radio and television. I thought about keeping quiet about that detail to preserve the mystery, but in the end came clean.

Does Dowie still speak today? Yes, in both a positive and negative sense. No matter how dark the world may seem – it is still God's world, and God is still in control. The gospel is just as powerful today in all of its fullness, including divine healing, as it ever was. We can and should keep praying that God will move in ever greater power in these Last Days in signs and wonders. We need Dowie's faith more today than ever before.

On a less positive note, it is a worrying trend that Dowie's mistakes are repeated in what is almost a race to the finish line regarding the Apocalypse. Many people claim to be a visionary or a prophet, revealing things that even Jesus in his earthly ministry, said he did not know. That should not be, and I hope by reading Dowie's story you have a better understanding of where that extra-Biblical teaching can lead.

Of course, there are true apostles and prophets, and we can thank God for them. But God doesn't need any human being to direct his end-time dealing with our world. He is perfectly capable of doing that himself. He doesn't need any prompts, or any more "preparing of the way," than preaching the gospel in all its fullness, living and praying in line with the Word of God.

I want to end on a note that gives me great confidence, though it may sound incongruous given my earlier comments. God does reveal his plans to his prophets and the prophecy of the end-time outpouring of the Holy Spirit, first given in Port Glasgow in 1830, can be traced in its fulfilment all the way down the generations to this day.

Dowie was a lynchpin in that, and for all his faults, I have a great respect for him. We are all imperfect people. While we live in the body, let's try to learn from the mistakes of the past. And let us not let go of our confidence - this same Jesus will come again.

These are just a few of 'God's Witnesses' to divine healing.

Mary Dowling,
healed of blindness

F.A. Graves,
healed of epilepsy

Jennie Lake, healed of
heart disease

Michael Lindskog, healed after bitten by
rabid dog

God's Witnesses to divine healing

May Lohman, healed of
lameness

H.S. Lehr, healed of
tuberculosis

Christina Knudson, healed
of consumption

James Bates, damaged knee
restored

God's Witnesses to divine healing

Elizabeth Reynolds, healed of consumption

Lucy Gaston, healed of kidney trouble

Cora Carley, healed of deafness

Sunshine Harding, healed of scarlet fever

243

God's Witnesses to divine healing

Alta Gertrude Newels, healed of lameness

Azro Rodgers, healed of cancer

Albion Wyman, healed of consumption

Claudia Thomas, healed of heart trouble

God's Witnesses to divine healing

Carlotta Benda, previously
deaf and dumb

Linda Karch, healed of
deafness

Clara Hoeft,
healed of lameness

Lydia Markley,
leg lengthened

245

God's Witnesses to divine healing

Annie Miller, rheumatism

Ethel Post, healed of cancer

Charles O Davis, leg lengthened

Emma Parker, fluid retention

God's Witnesses to divine healing

Jennie Brown, rheumatism

Herman Petersen, bowel inflammation

Lulu Dayton, tuberculosis of bowels

Sadie Cody, healed of backbone disease

God's Witnesses to divine healing

Samuel Nelson, cured of tapeworm

Pearl Irish, healed of hip disease

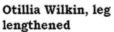

Otillia Wilkin, leg lengthened

Mary Casey - healed of cancer

God's Witnesses to divine healing

R F Palm, healed of cancer

Theodore Nelson, healed of typhoid fever

M.A. Cook, healed of vertigo

Mrs Smythe, healed of consumption

God's Witnesses to divine healing

Officer Vettin, son healed of rheumatism

Henry Bussian, son healed of appendicitus

Gustav Wolter, healed of rheumatism

Officer Anderson, healed of rheumatism

Excerpted from Leaves of Healing

Artist Charles Champe at work in his studio

Escaping to the City of Refuge

Zion's vision of the Blessed Hope

Zion's witness against adulterers

Humbly submitting to the Devil's will

**Methodism and the Dowie
teachings have nothing in common**

Apostate Salvation Army

The Masonic Covenant revealed

Zion's conflict with apostate churches

Zion confronts the modern Pharaoh

Elijah nailing his thesis upon the door of apostate Lutheranism

g

257

Zion confronting the horns of an apostate church

Zion smites sin, the cause of disease

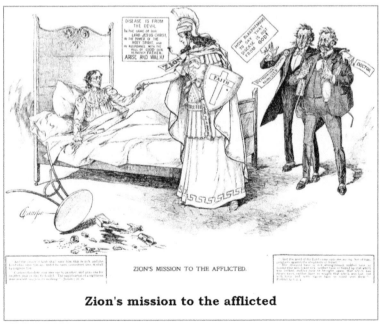

Zion's mission to the afflicted

Why the medical missionary hates Zion

Zion's witness against oppressors

Zion's buzzsaw and the ridiculous mice

Zion's discovery of Masonic bedfellows

BIBLIOGRAPHY

Bennett, David Malcolm, *Edward Irving Reconsidered: The Man, His Controversies and the Pentecostal Movement* (Eugene, OR: Wipf & Stock), 2014.

Blaikie, William, G., *Thomas Chalmers* (Edinburgh & London: Oliphant, Anderson & Ferrier), 1896.

Boase, C.W., *The Elijah Ministry, The Tokens of its Ministry to the Christian Church* (Dundee: Robert Grant & Son), 1868.

Bonar, Andrew, *Narrative of a mission of inquiry to the Jews from the Church of Scotland in 1839* (Philadelphia: Presbyterian Board of Publication), 1845.

Bonar, Horatius, *Prophetic Journals* (1849-1873), (London: J. Nisbet).

Brumback, Carl, *Suddenly ... from Heaven, A History of the Assemblies of God* (Springfield, MO: Gospel Publishing House), 1861.

Burgess, Stanley (Ed) & Van Der Maas, Eduard M (Ass Ed), *The International Dictionary of Pentecostal and Charismatic Movements* (Grand Rapids Michigan: Zondervan), 2002.

Calderwood, Henry, *The Philosophy of the Infinite* (Edinburgh: Thomas Constable & Co), 1854.

Campbell, John McLeod, *The Nature of the Atonement* (London: MacMillan & Co.), 1873.

Chalmers, Thomas D, *The Christian and Civil Economy of Large Towns* (New York: Charles Scribner's Sons), 1900.

Cook, Philip L., Zion City Illinois, *Twentieth-Century Utopia* (New York: Syracuse University Press), 1996.

Darms, Anton (1938), *Life and Work of John Alexander Dowie* (Zion: The Christian Catholic Church), 1938.

Dorries, David, *Edward Irving's Incarnational Christology* (Fairfax, VA: Xulon), 2002.

Faupel D. William, *The Everlasting Gospel – The Significance of Eschatology in the Development of Pentecostal Thought* (Sheffield: Sheffield Academic Press), 1996.

Gall James, *The Carrubbers Close Mission* (Edinburgh: Gall & Inglis), 1860.

Haggard, Howard Wilcox, *Devils, Drugs and Doctors: The Story of the Science of Healing from Medicine Men to Doctor* (London: William Heinemann), 1913.

Harlan, Rolvix, *John Alexander Dowie and the Christian Catholic Apostolic Church in Zion* (Evansville: Robert. M. Antes), 1906.

Irving, Edward (foreword by Bonar, Horatius), *The Last Days* (London: James Nisbet & Co.), 1850.

Kelly, William (ed), *The Collected Writings of J. N. Darby*, Vol 6, (London: G. Morrish), undated.

Kiek, E.S., *An Apostle in Australia* (London: Independent Press Ltd), 1927.

Lake, John G. (ed Reidt, Wilford H.), *Adventures in God* (Tulsa, OK: Harrison House), 1981.

Lewis, George, *The Life Story of Aunt Janet* (Selkirk: James Lewis), 1902.

Liardon, Roberts, *God's Generals – Why They Succeeded and Why Some Failed* (Tulsa, OK: Albury), 1996.

Lindsay, Gordon, *The Sermons of John Alexander Dowie, Champion of the Faith* (Shreveport: Voice of Healing Publishing Company), 1951.

Lindsay, Gordon, *John Alexander Dowie, A Life Story of Trials, Tragedies and Triumphs* (Dallas, Texas: Christ for the Nations), 1980.

MacKenzie, Kenneth, *Our Physical Heritage in Christ* (Fleming New York: H. Revell & Co.), 1923.

Newcomb, Arthur, *Dowie, Anointed of the Lord* (New York: Century), 1930.

Oliphant, Margaret, *The Life of Edward Irving, Minister of the National Scotch Church, London* (London: Hurst & Blackett), 1862.

Petersen, Ephraim, *An Ideal City for an Ideal People* (Publisher not stated), 1905.

Pietrusza David, *Judge and Jury: The Life and Times of Judge Kenesaw Mountain Landis* (South Bend, Ind: Diamond Communications), 1998.

Rice, S., *Divine Healing as Taught by Rev. John Alex. Dowie Refuted and his Work Exposed* (Chicago: Stansbury McCormick & Co Printers), 1896.

Robinson, James, *Theological Roots in the Transatlantic World 1830-1880* (Eugene, OR: Pickwick), 2013.

Robinson, James, *Divine Healing: The Holiness-Pentecostal Transition Years, 1890-1906* (Eugene, OR: Pickwick), 2013.

Ross James, *A History of Congregational Independency in Scotland* (Glasgow: James MacLehose & Sons), 1900.

Sheldrake, Edna, *The Personal Letters of John Alexander Dowie* (Zion City: Wilbur Glenn Voliva), 1912.

Simpson, A. B., *The Four-Fold Gospel* (New York: Christian Alliance Publishing), 1890.

Stead, William T., *If Christ Came to Chicago* (London: Review of Reviews Office), 1894.

Story, Robert Herbert, *Memoir of the Reverend Robert Story* (Cambridge: MacMillan & Co.), 1862.

Tomlinson, Homer, A., *Diary of A. J. Tomlinson* (New York: Church of God, World Headquarters), 1949.

Torrance Thomas F., *Scottish Theology: From John Knox to John McLeod Campbell* (Edinburgh: T & T Clark), 1996.

Tozer, A.W. (1943), *Wingspread, Albert B. Simpson, a Study in Spiritual Altitude* (Harrisburg, PA: Christian Publications), 1943.

Woodsworth-Etter, *Maria Beulah, Acts of the Holy Ghost* (Dallas, Texas: John F. Worley Printing Co.), undated.

Wight, Ninian, *Memoir of the Rev. Henry Wight, by his Son* (Edinburgh: Edmiston & Douglas), 1862.

Wilks, Washington, *Edward Irving, An Ecclesiastical and Literary Biography* (London; William Freeman), 1854.

Wilson, William, *Memorials of Robert Smith Candlish* (Edinburgh: Adam & Black), 1880.

Various, *The Conversion of the Jews, a Series of Lectures by Ministers of the Church of Scotland* (Edinburgh: John Johnstone), 1842.

Historical and theological articles

Baer Jonathan R, 'Redeemed Bodies, The Functions of Divine Healing in Incipient Pentecostalism', *Church History*, Vol 70, No 4, 735-771.

Blumhofer, Edith, 'A Pentecostal Branch Grows in Dowie's Zion', *Heritage* Vol 6, No 3, 1986.

Boardman, W. E., *Record of the International Conference on Divine Healing and True Holiness held at the Agricultural Hall* (London: Snow), 1885.

Boddy, Alexander, 'A Visit to Zion City', *Confidence*, Vol 6, No 2, 1918.

Buckley, J., 'Dowie Analysed and Classified', *Century Illustrated Magazine*, (New York: The Century Co.), 1902.

Chant, Barry 'The Australian Career of John Alexander Dowie.' Paper presented to the Centre for the Study of Australian Christianity, 1992.

Chapman, Diana, 'The role of Woman in Early Pentecostalism', *Journal of the European Pentecostal Association*, Vol. XXVIII No. 2, Paternoster Periodicals, 2008.

Faupel D. William, 'Theological Influences on the Teaching and Practices of John Alexander Dowie', *Pneuma* 29, 2007.

Faupel D. William, 'The Missionary Strategy of John Alexander Dowie', *Wesleyan Theological Journal* Vol 42, No 1, 2007.

Gardiner, Colin P, 'Story of John Alexander Dowie', *Bread of Life*, Vol 6, No 3, 1957.

Gloege, Timothy E. W. 'Faith Healing, Medical Regulation and Public Religion in Progressive Era Chicago', *Religion and American Culture*, Vol. 23, No 2, 2013.

Grass, Tim, 'The Taming of the Prophets', *Journal of the European Pentecostal Association* Vol XVI, 1996.

Halsey, John J, 'The Genesis of a Modern Prophet', *American Journal of Sociology*, Vol 9, No 3, 1903.

Heath, Alden R, 'Apostle in Zion', *Journal of the Illinois State Historical Society* Vol 70, No 2, 1977.

Hein, Jennifer, 'A crisis of leadership: John Alexander Dowie and the Salvation Army in South Australia', *Journal of the Historical Society of South Australia*, No 39, 2011.

Hubbard, Elbert (ed Bert Hubbard), 'John Alexander Dowie' in *Selected Writings of Elbert Hubbard; his Mintage* Vol 5 (New York: W. H. Wise & Co.), 1922.

Illinois Circuit Court Reports, 3. 'Samuel Stevenson vs. John Alexander Dowie', (Chicago: T. H. Flood), 1909.

Lowe, Jason, 'John Alexander Dowie –A Modern Elijah', The *American Magazine*, 1902.

Murray, Andrew, 'Thomas Guthrie, Preacher and Philanthropist', Article available online at-https://banneroftruth.org/uk/resources/articles/2013/thomas-guthrie- preacher-and-philanthropist/

Swain J., 'John Alexander Dowie, 'The Prophet and his Profits', *Century Illustrated Magazine* (New York: The Century Co.), 1902.

Stanley, Brian, 'Edinburgh and World Christianity', *Studies in World Christianity* Vol. 17, Issue 1, 2011.

Synan, Vinson, 'A Healer in the House - A Historical Perspective on Healing in the Pentecostal / Charismatic Tradition', *Asian Journal of Pentecostal Studies*, 3/2, 2000.

Taylor, Malcolm John, 'Publish and be blessed: a case study in early Pentecostal publishing' PhD thesis, University of Birmingham, 1994.

Van der Laan, Cornelis, 'Discerning the Body: An Analysis of Pentecostalism in the Netherlands', *European Pentecostal Theological Association*, Vol 14/1, 1995

Various, *The Morning Watch*, (London: James Nisbet), 1832.

Wacker, Grant, 'Marching to Zion', Parts 1 & 2. *Heritage* Vol 6, No 2 & 3, 1996.

Publications by Dowie

Rome's Polluted Springs (Sydney: William Maddock), 1877.

The Drama, The Press and the Pulpit (Sydney: Jarrett & Co.), 1879.

Spiritualism Unmasked (Melbourne: George Robertson), 1882.

Sin in the camp, being an account of nine months work in the tabernacle, Sackville Street, Collingwood and a vindication of character (Melbourne: Henry Cooke), 1882.

Record of the Fifth Annual Convention (Melbourne: M. L. Hutchinson), 1887.

American Firstfruits (San Francisco: Leaves of Healing Office), 1889.

Zion's Holy War Against the Host of Hell in Chicago (Chicago: Zion Publishing House), 1900.

The Zion Banner (Chicago: Zion Printing & Publishing House), weekly, 1901.

Leaves of Healing (Chicago: Zion Printing & Publishing House),

1894-1906.

'Doctors, Drugs and Devils', *A Voice from Zion*, Vol 1, No 10 (Chicago: Zion Publishing House), 1897.

'What Should a Christian do When Sick?' *A Voice from Zion*, Vol 2, No 1 (Chicago: Zion Publishing House), 1898.

'Organisation of the Christian Catholic Church', *A Voice from Zion*, Vol 2, No 2 (Chicago: Zion Publishing House), 1898.

'You Dirty Boy', *A Voice from Zion*, Vol 2, No 3 (Chicago: Zion Publishing House), 1898.

'How to Pray', *A Voice from Zion*, Vol 2, No 4 (Chicago: Zion Publishing House), 1898.

'Christ's Method of Healing', *A Voice from Zion*, Vol 2, No 5 (Chicago: Zion Publishing House), 1898.

'Swine's Flesh', *A Voice from Zion*, Vol 2, No 6 (Chicago: Zion Publishing House), 1898.

'Tobacco – Satan's Consuming Fire', *A Voice from Zion*, Vol 2, No 7 (Chicago: Zion Publishing House), 1898.

'False Christian Science Unmasked', *A Voice from Zion*, Vol 2, No 8 (Chicago: Zion Publishing House), 1898.

'Divine Healing Vindicated', *A Voice from Zion*, Vol 2, No 9 (Chicago: Zion Publishing House), 1898.

'The Press- The Tree of Good and Evil', *A Voice from Zion*, Vol 2, No 10 (Chicago: Zion Publishing House), 1898.

'Estimates and Realities', *A Voice from Zion*, Vol 2, No 11 (Chicago: Zion Publishing House), 1898.

'Diabolical Spiritualism Unmasked', *A Voice from Zion*, Vol 2, No 12 (Chicago: Zion Publishing House), 1898.

Notes

1. The bairn sings

1. *Leaves of Healing* 6: 631.
2. Sheldrake, *Letters*, 13.
3. Sheldrake, *Letters*, 13.
4. *Leaves of Healing* 2: 466.
5. Sheldrake, *Letters*, 13.
6. Halsey, 'The Genesis of a Modern Prophet', 310.
7. 'Tobacco – Satan's Consuming Fire', 20-21. The Crags are part of Holyrood Park with the *Cat Nick* a cleft in the rock near the top at the highest point.
8. 'Tobacco – Satan's Consuming Fire', 21.
9. 'Tobacco – Satan's Consuming Fire', 21.
10. 'Tobacco – Satan's Consuming Fire', 21.
11. *Leaves of Healing* 7: 687.
12. *Leaves of Healing* 3: 585.
13. *Leaves of Healing* 3: 585.
14. *Leaves of Healing* 3: 585.
15. *Leaves of Healing* 7: 653.
16. *Leaves of Healing* 12: 817.
17. *Leaves of Healing* 12: 817.
18. *Leaves of Healing* 1: 760.
19. *Leaves of Healing* 1: 760.
20. *Leaves of Healing* 12: 817.
21. *Leaves of Healing* 12: 817.
22. *Leaves of Healing* 12: 817.
23. *Leaves of Healing* 12: 817.
24. Sheldrake, *Letters*, 333-334. Dowie believed he was the descendant of the clan "MacDhui" (*Leaves of Healing* 8: 65) and that these Highlanders were descended from the lost tribes of Israel. He cited his "old friend" Professor Blackie as support in this (*Leaves of Healing* 8: 180).
25. *Leaves of Healing* 1: 760
26. *Leaves of Healing* 16: 634.
27. MacKenzie, *Physical Heritage*, 20.
28. Synan, 'A Healer in the House', 90.

29. *Leaves of Healing* 12: 817
30. Wight, *Memoir of the Rev. Henry Wight*, 14. See also Henry Wight's obituary in *The Scottish Congregational Magazine* 1861, 267-271.
31. Oliphant, *Life of Edward Irving*, 275-276; Dorries, *Incarnational Christology*, 44.
32. Oliphant, *Life of Edward Irving*, 275.
33. Wight, *Memoir of the Rev. Henry Wight*, 34-36. For a useful summary of the Port Glasgow outpouring see Robinson, *Theological Roots in the Transatlantic World* and for Edward Irving see Bennett, *Edward Irving Reconsidered: The Man, His Controversies*, and Dorries, *Edward Irving's Incarnational Christology*.
34. See Grass 'The Taming of the Prophets.' Grass questions if 'Irvingism' "was ever a homogenous movement," given the marked differences between the London-based Apostles and the Presbyterian prophets who claimed direct inspiration from God. This is an important distinction, as the assumption is often made that Irving's theology equates to that of the Catholic Apostolic Church. In fact, Irving tried to straddle the two sides and died before much of the Catholic Apostolic Church doctrine was developed.
35. Story, *Memoir of the Reverend Robert Story*, 226.
36. Wight, *Memoir of the Reverend Henry Wight*, 37.
37. *The Sessional Papers Printed by Order of the House of Lords, Session 1837*; Ross, *History of Congregational Independency*, 230.
38. *Leaves of Healing* 1:39; Sheldrake, *Letters*, 13; *Ballarat Star*, 31 October 1903, 7.
39. *Leaves of Healing* 2: 466.
40. *Leaves of Healing* 2: 466.
41. Lewis, *The Life Story of Aunt Janet*, 48-49.
42. *Leaves of Healing* 12: 817. For a summary of McLeod Campbell's views, see Torrance, *Scottish Theology*, 287-8. McLeod Campbell wrote his best-known work on Atonement in 1856, around the same time Dowie dates hearing discussions on the doctrine of election.
43. See for instance, *Leaves of Healing* 1: 373 - "We are his off-spring and we share his nature," and *Leaves of Healing* 8: 240 for the Fatherhood of God. See also Dorries, *Edward Irving's Incarnational Christology*, 45 -"All of the works of Christ were done by the man anointed with the Holy Ghost, and not by the God mixing himself with the man...and the end of the whole mystery of his

incarnation is to show unto mortal men what every one of them, through faith in his name shall be able to perform."

44. See note 2:29 below for a discussion of Faupel's views on influences on Dowie.

45. John Nelson Darby visited Port Glasgow in July 1830 and refers to "a minister of an independent or some dissenting church in Edinburgh, then a church elder." (Kelly, *Collected Writings* Vol 6, 448-450). This is supported by Wight's son's Memoir of his father which places him in Port Glasgow at this time. It has been the subject of intense debate amongst Brethren writers as to whether Darby's end time views were influenced at that time. Taken in the round, likely not, but this is beyond the scope of this study.

46. *Leaves of Healing* 1: 373.

47. *Leaves of Healing* 1: 373.

48. *Leaves of Healing* 16: 766-767.

49. *Leaves of Healing* 16: 766-767.

50. *Leaves of Healing* 16: 766-767.

51. In *Leaves of Healing* 12: 783 Dowie referred to the desolation he saw as a boy when the 'Black Watch' returned to Edinburgh after the Crimean War.

52. *Holy War*, 48.

53. Sheldrake, *Letters*, 13.

54. *Leaves of Healing* 8: 141.

2. The student

1. Chant, 'The Australian Career of John Alexander Dowie', 1-2.

2. *Leaves of Healing* 8: 141; Harlan, *John Alexander Dowie*, 28.

3. Harlan, *John Alexander Dowie*, 28-29.

4. Harlan, *John Alexander Dowie*, 29.

5. *Leaves of Healing* 3: 104.

6. *Zion's Holy War*, 48.

7. *Leaves of Healing* 8: 142.

8. E. S. Kiek, *Apostle in Australia*, 297.

9. Chant, 'The Australian Career of John Alexander Dowie', 2.

10. 'Divine Healing Vindicated', 28. Elsewhere Dowie dated this as happening around 1864 (*Leaves of Healing* 8:179; *Leaves of Healing* 16: 175-176). It is difficult to tell how ill Dowie actually was at that time, as he obviously held down a job. In 1891 he described his condition as "given up by the medical

fraternity to die" (*Pittsburg Dispatch*, 5 November 1891, 2).

11. *Leaves of Healing* 16: 176.

12. Kiek, *Apostle in Australia*, 297.

13. Dowie was listed at the Faculty of Arts from 1869-1871 studying Latin, Greek, Logic and Moral Philosophy. He also studied in "theological halls" (Harlan, *John Alexander Dowie*, 29).

14. *Leaves of Healing* 1: 249; 6: 398-399.

15. 'Holy Willie' was based on Willie Fisher, an elder in Mauchline Church. According to Burns, Fisher was a hypocrite who spied on people and reported them to the minister if he thought they were doing wrong, but as Fisher was one of 'the elect' he excused his own immoral behaviour.

16. *Leaves of Healing* 3: 106.

17. *Leaves of Healing* 3: 106.

18. Harlan, *John Alexander Dowie*, 29. See also 'False Christian Science Unmasked', 16.

19. *Leaves of Healing* 8: 240.

20. *Leaves of Healing* 14: 554.

21. According to Simpson, a man had more chance of surviving the Battle of Waterloo than a surgical operation due to poor practice in hospitals of the day. Simpson is remembered at the Simpson Centre for Reproductive Medicine at the Royal Infirmary. Edinburgh, cited by NHS Lothian, Scotland's busiest maternity unit - see
http://www.nhslothian.scot.nhs.uk/OurOrganisation/AboutUs/OurHistory/Pa ges/default.aspx.

22. *Leaves of Healing* 3: 572.

23. *Leaves of Healing* 14: 554.

24. *Leaves of Healing* 16: 276.

25. *Leaves of Healing* 16:177, 201- 204; 12: 237-238.

26. *Leaves of Healing* 16:177.

27. *Leaves of Healing* 16: 177.

28. *Leaves of Healing* 16: 177.

29. In 'Theological Influences' Faupel sees three key strands theological strands as influential on Dowie – Edward Irving, the Mormons and the Holiness movement. Irving's eschatological views were clearly a factor by Dowie's own admission and his use of prophetic titles, as Faupel points out, "consistent with this worldview" ('Theological Influences', 227). Less

convincing are Faupel's views on the extent of the effect of the Mormons and the Holiness tradition. Dowie was nothing, if not his own man. He didn't "join" groups – he set them up. So it is unlikely Dowie seriously entertained joining the Mormons as "Plan C" if everything else fell through ('Theological Influences', 243). Additionally, it is unclear to what extent Dowie was actually influenced by the Holiness tradition or merely drew his support base from that group and adapted his message in line with that. In 'Stevenson v Dowie' a letter is referenced in which Dowie claimed Boardman did significant damage to the divine healing movement by writing that holiness must precede healing, a central tenet of Holiness thought (Stevenson vs Dowie, 1902, 158). This does not entirely equate with Faupel's claim that Dowie "took the Keswick doctrine of sanctification and applied it on a cosmic scale" ('Theological Influences', 241). 'Repentance should proceed healing' was probably a better description of Dowie's position, than 'holiness should proceed healing.' Overall, Dowie presents as more theologically eclectic than Faupel allows for, and weight should be given to his father John Murray Dowie's statement in 1903, that Dowie was, "only a Calvinist with a lot of faith healing egotism and new-fangled ideas grafted on" (*Rock Island Argus*, 21 November 1903, 10). Some of those ideas proved good, others less so.

30. Andrew Murray, 'Thomas Guthrie, Preacher and Philanthropist' – available online at https://banneroftruth.org/uk/resources/articles/2013/thomas-guthrie-preacher-and-philanthropist/.

31. Blaikie, *Thomas Chalmers*, 9. Although he didn't hold to some Irving's later views, notably, it was Chalmers who gave Edward Irving his first job as his associate minister in Glasgow.

32. *Leaves of Healing* 1: 69.

33. 'Diabolical Spiritualism Unmasked', 12.

34. Wilson, *Memorials of Robert Smith Candlish*, 30.

35. Candlish, in 'The Conversion of the Jews', 173.

36. Candlish, 'The Conversion of the Jews', 187.

37. See Andrew Bonar, *Narrative of a Mission of Inquiry*.

38. Horatius Bonar in particular wrote extensively on Irving and the practice of the gifts in Irving's church, but reserved judgment as to whether the 'manifestations' (i.e. speaking in tongues) were genuine due to the division produced. He did not discount the practice of spiritual gifts but was not

convinced what he saw was always genuine.

39. 'Elijah's Coming before the great and dreadful day of the Lord' (*Prophetic Journals*, 16, 1865).

40. Horatius Bonar, 'The Jew' in *Prophetic Journals*, 22, 1870, 214-216.

41. 'The Press, The Tree of Good and Evil', 10. Duncan would have been a particular favourite for Dowie. According to Duncan, "Hyper-Calvinism is all house and no door: Arminianism is all door and no house."

42. *Waterloo Daily Courier*, 15 June 1906, 7.

43. *Leaves of Healing* 6: 398-399.

44. *Leaves of Healing* 6: 392.

45. *Leaves of Healing*, 6: 398-399.

46. *New York Sun*, 23 June 1906, 1.

3. Pastor Dowie

1. *Leaves of Healing* 16: 204.

2. Sheldrake, *Letters*, 24.

3. Sheldrake, *Letters*, 24.

4. Sheldrake, *Letters*, 25. The *Adelaide Observer* reported membership in Alma had dropped to below 10 during the period Dowie was in office. Attendees varied from 15-50. £60 had been raised during that period, including the denominational grant (*Adelaide Observer*, 12 April 1873, 4).

5. Sheldrake, *Letters*, 37.

6. Sheldrake, *Letters*, 38.

7. Sheldrake, *Letters*, 38.

8. Sheldrake, *Letters*, 49-50.

9. Sheldrake, *Letters*, 64.

10. Sheldrake, *Letters*, 64.

11. Sheldrake, *Letters*, 70.

12. Sheldrake, *Letters*, 70.

13. Sheldrake, *Letters*, 32-33.

14. Sheldrake, *Letters*, 33.

15. Sheldrake, *Letters*, 43-45. The Australian press carried an obituary for Candlish. Although here Dowie does not identify Candlish by name in *Letters*, the quote he later gives when he recounts the story is from 'Sowers and Reapers' a sermon in Candlish's memoirs (*Leaves of Healing* 1: 69-70).

Elsewhere he refers to him as "Principal of the Free Church College" ('Spiritualism Unmasked', 12). See also *Leaves of Healing* 6: 538.
16. Sheldrake, *Letters*, 43-45.
17. *Leaves of Healing* 1: 69.
18. 'Spiritualism Unmasked', 13.
19. Sheldrake, *Letters*, 55.
20. Sheldrake, *Letters*, 58.
21. Sheldrake, *Letters*, 58.
22. Sheldrake, *Letters*, 85.
23. Kiek, *Apostle in Australia*, 297.
24. Sheldrake, *Letters*, 85.
25. Sheldrake, *Letters*, 71.
26. Sheldrake, *Letters*, 72.
27. Sheldrake, *Letters*, 74.
28. Sheldrake, *Letters*, 81.

4. Mary

1. There are various accounts of incident. The earliest is in Sheldrake when Dowie wrote to his parents in April 1876 and told them of burying 25 people from his congregation (Sheldrake, *Letters*, 96). This chapter is based on *Leaves of Healing* 16: 206-208. Sickness appears to have returned to Newtown in 1878 (Sheldrake, *Letters*, 160).

5. Jeanie and Dowie

1. *Leaves of Healing* 16: 208.
2. Sheldrake, *Letters*, 113.
3. Sheldrake, *Letters*, 139.
4. Sheldrake, *Letters*, 131.
5. Sheldrake, *Letters*, 136.
6. Sheldrake, *Letters*, 137.
7. Sheldrake, *Letters*, 138.
8. Sheldrake, *Letters*, 131.
9. Sheldrake, *Letters*, 127. In 1906, Gladstone implied Dowie had some sort of affair at that time. See note 15: 56
10. Sheldrake, *Letters*, 141.

11. Sheldrake, *Letters*, 143.

12. Sheldrake, *Letters*, 151.

13. Sheldrake, *Letters*, 177.

14. *Rome's Polluted Springs*, 3.

15. Kiek believed Dowie was becoming unbalanced even at that time. The Newtown Congregation were "in no way deserving of Dowie's violent strictures," (Kiek, *Apostle in Australia*, 297). However the frustration Dowie felt was a theme that ran throughout his ministry in the Congregational Church.

16. Kiek, *Apostle in Australia*, 297.

17. Sheldrake, *Letters*, 207.

18. Sheldrake, *Letters*, 238.

19. Sheldrake, *Letters*, 246.

20. Sheldrake, *Letters*, 206-207.

21. Sheldrake, *Letters*, 206.

22. Sheldrake, *Letters*, 132.

23. Sheldrake, *Letters*, 183-184.

24. Dowie's father stepped in with £100 to pay for new furniture (Sheldrake, *Letters*, 208).

25. Sheldrake, *Letters*, 210.

26. Sheldrake, *Letters*, 253.

27. Sheldrake, *Letters*, 220.

28. *Sydney Morning Herald*, 13 December 1879, 3; *Freeman's Journal* (Sydney) 20 December 1879, 16.

29. *Adelaide Observer*, 3 January 1880, 11.

30. Sheldrake, *Letters*, 266.

31. Sheldrake, *Letters*, 255.

32. Sheldrake, *Letters*, 278.

33. Sheldrake, *Letters*, 279.

34. Sheldrake, *Letters*, 281.

35. *Newcastle Morning Herald & Mining Advocate*, 24 June 1880, 2.

36. The Salvation Army's John Plumber claimed Dowie's church committee approached him when Dowie asked for advance funds on the strength of Holding's money. Plumber discovered Holding was the ex-employee of his brother-in-law in England and claimed to warn Dowie of Holding's identity on a number of occasions but Dowie refused to listen ('John Alexander Dowie

– the Story of a Bogus Fortune' *Observer* (Adelaide), 1 June 1907, 37).

37. *Sydney Morning Herald*, 1 September 1880, 6. See also Sheldrake, *Letters,* 257-265.

38. *The Age* (Melbourne), 9 January 1886, 15.

39. Sheldrake, *Letters*, 290-297. See also 'The Holding Imposture – Letter from Rev J A Dowie', *Christian Colonist*, 29 January 1886, 6.

40. Lindsay, *John Alexander Dowie*, 43.

41. Dowie said he forgave Holding and would not return to Sydney to press charges (*Christian Colonist*, 29 January 1886, 6).

42. 'John Alexander Dowie – The Story of a Bogus Fortune', *Observer* (Adelaide), 1 June 1907, 37.

43. Chant, 'The Australian Career of John Alexander Dowie', 10-11 no.53.

44. *Leaves of Healing* 15: 137.

[45]. *South Australian Register*, 4 August 1881, 6.

[46]. *Maitland Mercury & Hunter River General Advertiser*, 27 June 1882, 6.

[47]. Sheldrake, *Letters*, 307.

48. *Sin in the Camp*, 71.

49. Lindsay, *John Alexander Dowie*, 50. Lindsay did not appear to be aware of Dowie's earlier publication. *Sin in the Camp*. Cherbury's side of the story can be found in *The Argus* (Melbourne), 3 March 1883, 13.

50. *Sin in the Camp*, 78. A similar altercation took place between Dowie and a Captain Sutherland during Dowie's time with the Salvation Army (See also Hein, 'A Crisis of Leadership', 2011). *Sin in the Camp* contains several inconsistencies, notably, Dowie's claim to have established a large church in Alma that he gave up this post due to ill health (*Sin in the Camp*, 5).

51. *Sin in the Camp*, 84.

52. *Sin in the Camp*, 99.

6. Signs and wonders

1. *Against Spiritualism*, Introduction, xiii.

2. *Against Spiritualism*, Introduction, xiii.

3. 'Modern Miracles', *Mercury & Weekly Courier*, 15 September 1883; 3. See also *Express & Telegraph* (Adelaide) 3 May 1884, 3 and South Australian Register, 22 May 1884, 7.

4. *South Australian Register*, 22 May 1884, 7.

5. *Mercury & Weekly Courier*, 15 September 1883, 3; *South Australian Register*, 22 May 1884, 7.

6. *South Australian Register*, 22 May 1884, 7.

7. *South Australian Register*, 22 May 1884, 7.

8. *Port Adelaide News*, 2 May 1884, 1.

9. *Ballarat Star*, 9 October 1884, 4.

10. *Ballarat Star*, 20 December, 1884, 2.

11. *Ballarat Star*, 9 October 1884, 4.

12. *Ballarat Star*, 9 October 1884, 4.

13. *Ballarat Star*, 7 October 1884, 4.

14. Sheldrake, *Letters*, 332.

15. Boardman, *Record of the International Conference*, 171-175.

16. Goethe (trans. by Thomas Carlyle), cited in Dowie's account of his vision (*Leaves of Healing* 1:6; 6:335-336.)

17. *Leaves of Healing* 1: 6.

18. *Leaves of Healing* 1: 45.

19. *Ballarat Star*, 17 March 1885, 2.

20. *Mercury and Weekly Courier*, 24 April 1885, 2.

21. *Ballarat Star*, 22 May 1885, 4; *Adelaide Observer*, 9 May 1885, 31. The land was purchased from a Mr Thomson, one of Dowie's supporters for £1567, on a lease agreement with an option to buy. The church was built at a cost of £1750 – paid for by subscriptions. A change to the terms of the lease led to Thomson evicting the church from the premises until he got his money (*The Age* (Melbourne), 29 May 1885, 7.

22. *Mercury & Weekly Courier*, 8 May 1885, 2.

23. *Maitland Mercury & Hunter River*, 7 May 1885, 7; *Newcastle Morning Herald & Miners' Advocate*, 9 May, 1885, 7.

24. *Evening News* (Adelaide) 7 May 1885, 8. A similar dispute took place three years before when Dowie lodged an unsuccessful prosecution against the Police Commissioner (*Express & Telegraph Adelaide*, 4 August 1881, 3.)

25. *Daily Telegraph*, 11 May 1885, 3.

26. *Leader* (Melbourne), 30 May 1885, 28.

27. *Sydney Mail and New South Wales Advertiser*, 4 July 1885, 42.

28. *Argus* (Melbourne), 12 June 1885, 6; *North Eastern Ensign*, 19 June 1885, 2.

29. *Christian Colonist*, 5 March, 1886, 4.
30. Sheldrake, *Letters*, 326.
31. The life insurance policy is a curious detail but seemed to be because Dowie genuinely feared for his life and still had debt outstanding in Sydney.
32. *Evening News*, Sydney, 4 September 1885, 6. Dowie's office was badly damaged but the overall church building only suffered minor damage.
33. Sheldrake, *Letters*, 326.
34. Sheldrake, *Letters*, 318.
35. Sheldrake, *Letters*, 313.
36. Sheldrake, *Letters*, 319.
37. Sheldrake, *Letters*, 319. Jeanie MacFarlane Dowie died in the early hours of 1 November 1885, immediately after one of Dowie's healing crusades to Ballarat. For her obituary see *Argus* (Melbourne), 2 November 1885, 1.
38. Sheldrake, *Letters*, 320.
39. In *Leaves of Healing*, 3: 609, Dowie implies his daughter's death was the result of epilepsy brought on by demonic attack and elsewhere that he had a "devil of dyspepsia" (*Leaves of Healing* 16: 175).
40. *Leaves of Healing*, 3: 609.
41. Sheldrake, *Letters*, 321.
42. *Leaves of Healing*, 1: 45.
43. *Leaves of Healing*, 1: 46.
44. *Christian Colonist*, 5 March 1886, 4.
45. *Leaves of Healing*, 3: 257.
46. Sheldrake, *Letters*, 333.
47. Sheldrake, *Letters*, 332.
48. Sheldrake, *Letters*, 334.
49. Sheldrake, *Letters*, 332.
50. *Record of the Fifth Annual Convention*, 18-19.
51. *Record of the Fifth Annual Convention*, 15.
52. *Record of the Fifth Annual Convention*, 15.
53. *Record of the Fifth Annual Convention*, 13.
54. *Record of the Fifth Annual Convention*, 16.
55. *Record of the Fifth Annual Convention*, 16.
56. *Record of the Fifth Annual Convention*, 36.
57. Sheldrake, *Letters*, 345.

58. *Christian Colonist*, 2 August 1889, 2.

7. American Firstfruits
1. Lindsay, Life of John Alexander Dowie, 63.
2. Lindsay, *Life of John Alexander Dowie*, 63.
3. *American Firstfruits*, 47.
4. *American Firstfruits*, 4.
5. *Leaves of Healing* 1: 149,187.
6. Lindsay, *Life of John Alexander Dowie*, 63.
7. *Leaves of Healing* 1:149.
8. *American Firstfruits*, 5.
9. *American Firstfruits*, 4.
10. *American Firstfruits*, 5.
11. *American Firstfruits*, 47.
12. *American Firstfruits*, 47
13. *American Firstfruits*, 80.
14. *American Firstfruits*, 11-12.
15. *American Firstfruits*, 12-13.
16. *American Firstfruits*, 13.
17. *Christian Colonist*, 2 August 1889, 2.
18. 'Talks with Ministers' 10, appendix to *American Firstfruits*.
19. Harlan, *John Alexander Dowie*, 146.
20. 'The Press: The Tree of Good and Evil', 14-15.
21. *American Firstfruits*, 3.
22. 'Divine Healing Vindicated', 17.
23. *Los Angeles Herald*, 7 June 1889, 2.
24. 'Divine Healing Vindicated', 4.
25. 'Divine Healing Vindicated', 19.
26. 'Divine Healing Vindicated', 26-27.
27. *Daily Alta* (California), 1 February 1889, 8.
28. *Leaves of Healing* 6: 1.
29. Tozer, *Wingspread*, 134.
30. *Leaves of Healing* 3: 763-767. According to Tozer, Dowie arranged a series of lectures to speak against Simpson but was forced to cancel them all when a fishbone stuck in his throat (Tozer, *Wingspread*, 135). The timing suggests the

invitation to minister at Western Springs, Chicago followed soon after.
31. *Leaves of Healing* 1: 382.
32. *Oakland Tribune*, 31 January 1890, 8.
33. MacKenzie, *Our Physical Heritage in Christ*, 22.
34. 'You Dirty Boy', 24; *Leaves of Healing* 1: 481-484.
35. Over the next few years, he preached in hired halls in Chicago and conducted missions to Canada, Maryland, Minnesota and Pennsylvania. (*Table Talk* (Melbourne, 27 February 1902. 18).
36. *Chicago Tribune*, February 27 1891, 3.

8. The little wooden hut
1. Murat Halstead quoted in *Chicago Tribune*, 8 October 1893.
2. See Stead, *If Christ Came to Chicago*.
3. *Chicago Tribune*, 8 October 1893.
4. *Table Talk* (Melbourne), 27 February 1902, 18.
5. *Leaves of Healing* 6: 2
6. In November 1893, Dowie agreed to run the work in Chicago as a Divine Healing Mission (*Leaves of Healing* 1: 478).
7. *Leaves of Healing* 6: 2.
8. *Leaves of Healing* 3: 434.
9. *Leaves of Healing* 6: 2.
10. *Leaves of Healing* 7: 369.
11. *Leaves of Healing* 7: 369.
12. *Leaves of Healing* 1: 60.
13. *Leaves of Healing* 1: 155.
14. *Leaves of Healing* 1: 14.
15. *Leaves of Healing* 1:6.
16. Rice, *Divine Healing as Taught by Rev. John Alex Dowie*, 17.
17. Stead, *If Christ Came to Chicago*, 9.
18. *Leaves of Healing* 1: 220. Dowie moved from this building to the Chicago Auditorium (*Chicago Tribune*, 30 April 1894, 9; Harlan, *John Alexander Dowie*, 34).
19. *Evening World* (New York), April 16 1894, 2.
20. 'Elijah's Restoration Messages of Purity, Peace and Power: Purification by Obedience', *Voice of Zion*, 28-29 in Heath, 'Apostle in Zion', 105.

21. *Leaves of Healing* 1: 193-195.
22. *Clinton Democrat*, 8 March, 1894, quoted in *Leaves of Healing* 1: 195.
23. Gardiner, *Story of John Alexander Dowie*, 12.
24. *Leaves of Healing* 8: 97-101.
25. *Leaves of Healing* 1: 370.
26. *Latter Rain Evangel*, May 1911, 19-22.
27. *American Firstfruits*, 3.
28. Taylor, 'Publish and Be Blessed', 64, note 28.
29. *Leaves of Healing* 8: 473.
30. *Leaves of Healing* 3: 742.
31. *Leaves of Healing* 9: 227.
32. Brumback, *History of the Assemblies of God*, 10.
33. *Leaves of Healing* 3: 611.
34. *Leaves of Healing* 4: 350-351.
35 *Leaves of Healing* 1: 385.
36 *Leaves of Healing* 1: 534.
37 Lake, 'How I came to devote my life to the ministry of healing', *Adventures in God*.
38 *Leaves of Healing* 1: 179.
39. *Leaves of Healing* 1: 33.
40. *Leaves of Healing* 1: 49.
41. *Leaves of Healing* 1: 235.
42. *Leaves of Healing* 1: 129.
43. *Leaves of Healing* 1: 81.
44. *Leaves of Healing* 1: 433, 353.

9. Year of persecution

1. Gloerge, 'Faith Healing', 189.
2. *Chicago Tribune*, 12 July 1895, 8.
3. *Chicago Tribune*, 27 April 1895, 1.
4. *Chicago Tribune*, 24 June 1895, 11.
5. *Chicago Tribune*, 25 December, 1894, 11.
6. *Chicago Tribune*, 23 April 1894.
7. Gloerge, 'Faith Healing', 196.
8. *Chicago Tribune*, 29 June 1894, 8.

9. *Chicago Tribune*, 9 January 1895, 8.

10. *Leaves of Healing* 1: 84.

11. *Leaves of Healing* 1: 519.

12. 'Doctors, Drugs and Devils' first printed in *Physical Culture*, April 1895, 81-86, reprinted in *A Voice from Zion* (October 1897).

13. *Leaves of Healing* 1: 520.

14. Stead, *If Christ Came to Chicago*, 152-153.

15. *Chicago Inter Ocean*, 7 June 1895, 1. H.H. Kohlsaat sold his interests in the *Chicago Inter Ocean* in 1894 and purchased the *Chicago Times Herald*.

16. *Chicago Tribune*, 14 June 1895, 1.

17. *Chicago Inter Ocean*, 2 July 2 1895, quoted in Gloerge, 'Faith Healing', 198.

18. *New York Evangelist*, 8 August 1895, 26 quoted in Gloerge, 'Faith Healing', 198.

19. *Chicago Tribune*, 12 July 1895, 6.

20. See Affidavits reprinted in *Leaves of Healing* 1: 678-713.

21. Lindsay, *Life of John Alexander Dowie*, 2. Lindsay's assessment that the lower courts were "dominated by his enemies" is supported by Stead's study of Chicago at that time. Stead claimed the police regularly fabricated evidence to make money out of those accused. (Stead, *If Christ Came to Chicago*, 294-308).

22. Dowie's court testimony reprinted in *Leaves of Healing* 1: 693.

23. Harlan, *John Alexander Dowie*, 34.

24. *Chicago Tribune*, 17 June 1895, 8.

25. *Chicago Tribune*, 23 July 1895, 6.

26. *Leaves of Healing* 1: 578.

27. Gloerge, 'Faith Healing', 200.

28. Gloerge, 'Faith Healing', 200.

29. Gloerge, 'Faith Healing', 200.

30. Gloerge states, beginning in 1890, the *Tribune* published a reported 450 articles on Dowie (Gloerge, 'Faith Healing', 189).

31. *Chicago Tribune*, 2 December 1903, 3.

10. The Christian Catholic Church

1. *Leaves of Healing* 6: 24.

2. "The church is catholic for it is Christ's own bride and the purchase of his

blood and that church is catholic because it is universal" ('Organisation of the Christian Catholic Church', 25). See also his 1877 work, *Rome's Polluted Springs*, refuting Rome's claim to Apostolic Succession.

3. 'Organisation of the Christian Catholic Church', 48.

4. 'Organisation of the Christian Catholic Church', 95.

5. *The Morning Watch*, 1832, 442.

6. *Leaves of Healing* 1: 479.

7. *Leaves of Healing* 16: 643. Dowie was dismissive of the Catholic Apostolic Church as "dead sacramentalism" although he maintained there are good people in it.

8. 'Organisation of the Christian Catholic Church', 77; *Leaves of Healing* 6: 392.

9. 'Organisation of the Christian Catholic Church', 37.

10. Since November 1893, Dowie held responsibility for finances in Zion Tabernacle. The money he raised appeared to have convinced him this was a more profitable model than individual Divine Healing Associations (*Leaves of Healing* 1: 478).

11 *Leaves of Healing* 6: 4.

12. *Leaves of Healing* 6: 4.

13. *Leaves of Healing* 3: Introduction, v.

14. *Leaves of Healing* 3: 488.

15. *Leaves of Healing* 16: 639.

16. *Leaves of Healing* 6: 400.

17. *Leaves of Healing* 6: 37.

18. *Leaves of Healing* 3: 450-451.

19. See http://www.chicagomag.com/Chicago-Magazine/February-2010/On-Joseph-R-Dunlops-Chicago-Dispatch/.

20. It has been suggested that Dowie prophesied McKinley's assassination. Dowie's comments came from observations that McKinley's security was lax when he witnessed an unhappy visitor put his hand on his hip pocket when told the President could not see him. Dowie thought it would be easy enough to pull a revolver out of it (*Leaves of Healing* 3: 451).

21. *Leaves of Healing* 6: 5.

22. *Leaves of Healing* 4:365-366.

23 *Leaves of Healing* 4: 201.

24. Dowie claimed that the identification of Christ as the Messenger of the

Covenant was due to a mistranslation of Malachi 3: 1 (*Leaves of Healing* 6: 361-362).

25. *Zion's Holy War*, 137.

26. *Zion's Holy War*, 137.

27. *Zion's Holy War*, 4.

28. *Zion's Holy War*, 9-10.

29. *Zion's Holy War*, 91-2.

30. *Zion's Holy War*, 94-95.

31. Zion's leaders later claimed Dowie drew on Zion Bank's funds from the beginning to pay personal debt. See note 12: 3.

32. Preached in Chicago Auditorium and published under 'State Board of Death' in Heath, 'Apostle in Zion', 108.

33. *Zion's Holy War*, 40.

34. *Chicago Daily Tribune*, 19 October 1899, 1.

35. *Leaves of Healing* 6: 12.

36. *Chicago Tribune*, 28 October 1899, 1.

37. *Chicago Tribune*, 1 November 1899, 1.

38. *Leaves of Healing* 5: 460-461.

39. *Chicago Tribune*, 3 October, 1899, 6.

40. *Evening Times*, Washington, 3 October 1899, 6

41. *Chicago Chronicle*, 2 October, 1899, 2. According to Dowie, the Chronicle "took up the cudgels the other day for Mr Torrey" (*Zion's Holy War*, 51).

42. *Chicago Tribune*, 3 October 1899, 6.

43. *Missouri Valley Times*, 5 October 1899, 3.

44. Moody believed in the possibility of divine healing but felt no compulsion "to practice it therapeutically" (Gloerge, 'Faith Healing',192).

45. *Zion's Holy War*, 53.

46. *Leaves of Healing* 6: 700.

47. *Leaves of Healing* 6: 699.

48. *Leaves of Healing* 6: 640.

49. *Leaves of Healing* 6: 699.

50. *Chicago Tribune*, 14 April 1900, 13. Dowie claimed Torrey made certain statements which Torrey then denied, stating he was not in Chicago when the statements were supposed to be made. Torrey admitted sending the letter but said this was at the urging of one of his family and his daughter had already

recovered by the time that Dowie received his letter. The timeline suggests Torrey's account is substantially correct.

51. Lindsay incorectly dated her death to 1882 and suggested at the time of little Jeanie's death, Dowie was "not prepared to enter, fully, into that ministry (of divine healing), but regarded it more or less as a special ministry that God had given during a time of emergency"(Lindsay, *John Alexander Dowie*, 47). This dating was incorrect, she died in 1885 - see note 6: 37. The sequence of letters in Sheldrake is misleading which could have led to Lindsay's mistake.

11. God's Own City

1. Owen was decried as demonically inspired by the Port Glasgow prophets. His first experiment in social engineering prior to building New Harmony was in New Lanark, around forty miles from Port Glasgow.

2. 'Joseph Smith's Plan for the City of Zion' - http://ldsmag.com/article-1-8673/.

3. The eschatological dimension of the early Pentecostals is noted by Faupel (*The Everlasting Gospel – The Significance of Eschatology in the Development of Pentecostal Thought*). Interestingly, Lindsay views eschatology as almost a later addition to Dowie's beliefs, a point at which, "his dreams became visionary" (Lindsay, *Life of John Alexander Dowie*, 4). Whilst admittedly Dowie's actions were extreme, Lindsay's comments do indicate the shift of the Pentecostal movement away from its eschatological roots.

4. *Leaves of Healing* 6: 244.

5. *Zion's Holy War*, 224.

6. *Zion's Holy War*, 269.

7. *Leaves of Healing* 11: 224, 606.

8. *Leaves of Healing* 4: 382.

9. *Leaves of Healing* 6: 339.

10. *Leaves of Healing* 6: 338.

11. *Leaves of Healing* 6: 338.

12. *Leaves of Healing* 6: 27.

13. *Zion Banner*, 18 December 1901, 497.

14. *Zion Banner*, 18 December 1901, 497.

15. *Logansport Journal*, 23 December 1900, 8.

16. *Leaves of Healing* 6: 677.

17. *Leaves of Healing* 1: 479.

18. *Leaves of Healing* 3: 394.

19. This became the motto of Dowie's 'Theocratic party' - see Harlan, *John Alexander Dowie*, 7.

20. *Leaves of Healing* 8: 500.

21. 'Organisation of the Christian Catholic Church', 37.

22. Faupel, 'Theological Influences on the Teachings and Practices of John Alexander Dowie', 235.

23. Harlan, *John Alexander Dowie*, 179.

24. Cook, *Zion City*, 46.

25. Wacker, 'Marching to Zion', Part 2, 10.

26. Lindsay, *Life of John Alexander Dowie*, 126.

27. *Leaves of Healing* 7: 393.

28. *Leaves of Healing* 7:397.

29. *Leaves of Healing* 7:397.

30. *Leaves of Healing* 7:397.

31. *Leaves of Healing* 7:398.

32. Newcomb, *Dowie, Anointed of the Lord*, 104.

33. *Leaves of Healing* 14: 278.

34. Lindsay, *Life of John Alexander Dowie*, Introduction.

35. 'Stevenson v Dowie',142-143. See also *Chicago Tribune*, 25 July 1900, 8.

36. *Leaves of Healing* 7: 521-522.

37. *Leaves of Healing* 6: 458.

38. Cook, *Zion City*, 35.

39. *Leaves of Healing* 7: 572.

12. Zion Uncovered

1. Hubbard, 'Dowie' 104. Hubbard was sceptical of any form of organised religion - "People who are able to do their own thinking should not allow others to do it for them lest their think pores close" (Hubbard, 'Dowie', 4).

2. *Logansport Journal*, 23 December 1900, 8.

3. *Rock Island Argus*, 28 June 1906, 1; *Chicago Tribune* 9 April 1906, 2. The *Boston Evening Transcript*, 25 April, 1906, 28 puts the initial sum at $50 000.

4. Polly Wigglesworth was baptised at this time – *Leaves of Healing* 8: 64. See Robinson, *Divine Healing: The Holiness-Pentecostal Transition Years* for links between the Wigglesworth and other British Holiness figures with Dowie.

5. *Chicago Tribune*, 28 November 1900, 9.
6. *San Francisco Call*, 27 November 1900, 2.
7. *Leaves of Healing* 8: 214.
8. *Leaves of healing* 8: 196.
9. *Leaves of Healing* 8: 471.
10. See Lindsay, *Life of John Alexander Dowie*, 143. Lindsay relates the impression held in Zion that Jeanie Dowie "lost her simplicity of life; that she bought gowns in Paris and indulged in extravagances."
11. According to Stevenson, this took place in May 1901. By November, Dowie called him "an apostate liar" who disposed of Mary Ann's body into the sea, so that no autopsy could take place (*Leaves of Healing* 10:120; 'Stevenson v Dowie', 192). The *Chicago Tribune* reported Stevenson became engaged to another woman in New York shortly after Mary Ann's death (*Chicago Tribune*, 16 March 1902, 7).
12. *Leaves of Healing* 9: 206.
13. *Leaves of Healing* 9: 722.
14. *Leaves of Healing* 9: 722.
15. 'Stevenson v Dowie', 139.
16. 'Stevenson v Dowie', 140.
17. 'Stevenson v Dowie', 146.
18. 'Stevenson v Dowie', 150.
19. Mary Ann also signed the private agreement – 'Stevenson v Dowie', 151.
20. 'Stevenson v Dowie', 152.
21. 'Stevenson v Dowie', 154-155, 176.
22. 'Stevenson v Dowie', 155.
23. 'Stevenson v Dowie', 196-197.
24. 'Stevenson v Dowie', 182.
25. 'Stevenson v Dowie', 181.
26. 'Stevenson v Dowie', 181.
27. 'Stevenson v Dowie', 193. In *Leaves of Healing* 6: 333, Dowie lists those who opposed him and died. Given the sheer volume of people Dowie argued with, the list is not particularly statistically significant!
28. 'Stevenson v Dowie', 188.
29. 'Stevenson v Dowie', 193.
30. 'Stevenson v Dowie', 186.
31. *San Francisco Call*, 29 December 1901, 20.

32. *Indianapolis Journal*, 27 December 1901, 3.
33. *Chicago Tribune*, 31 December 1901, 16.
34. *New York Tribune*, 22 December 1901, 5.
35. *San Francisco Call*, 1 February 1902, 2.
36. *San Francisco Call*, 1 February 1902, 2.
37. *Rock Island Argus*, 5 February 1902, 1.
38. *Leaves of Healing*11: 524.
39. *Leaves of Healing*11: 525.
40. *Leaves of Healing*11: 455.
41. Harlan, *John Alexander Dowie*, 9-10.
42. Harlan, *John Alexander Dowie*, 10.
43. Voliva's testimony given in court (*New York Times*, 21 June 1906, 5).
44. *St Paul Globe*, 9 December, 1903, 39; *Leaves of Healing* 10: 785
45. *Leaves of Healing* 10: 781-796.

13. Elijah must come

1. Harlan, *John Alexander Dowie*, 141-142.
2. *New York Times*, 3 June 1901.
3. *Chicago Tribune*, 3 June 1901, 3.
4. Lindsay, *Life of John Alexander Dowie*, 145, 148.
5. Lindsay, *Life of John Alexander Dowie*, 149.
6. *Chicago Tribune*, 3 June 1901, 3.
7. *Leaves of Healing* 9: 214.
8. *Leaves of Healing* 11: 605. Several different people appear to have said this to Dowie over the years. For example - a stranger he met when he was crossing the English Channel (*Leaves of Healing* 9: 198); a "Christian scholar" in Melbourne which led to a sudden revelation that his healing ministry must mean he was Elijah (*Leaves of Healing* 14: 50); in letters from an Evangelist Barnes of Florida (*Leaves of Healing* 7: 215, 756).
9. *Leaves of Healing* 11: 605. Dowie maintained she was "in the Kingdom," although she would not confess Christ due to her family.
10. *Leaves of Healing* 9: 216-217.
11. *Leaves of Healing* 9: 209.
12. When Dowie put this to his leaders 251 out of 254 agreed with three waverers (*Leaves of Healing* 9: 199).

13. *Leaves of Healing* 11: 591.

14. *Rock Island Argus*, 26 December 1903, 1; *Bureau County Tribune*, 1 January 1904, 4.

15. It is unclear if Dowie is perhaps referring to the light he saw in Australia, or if this is another occasion. There is no sense when he received the vision in Australia, he interpreted this as a sign he was Elijah but he may well have seen this significance at a later date.

16. *Leaves of Healing* 9: 238.

17. *Leaves of Healing* 8: 787.

18. *Leaves of Healing* 8: 787.

19. *Chicago Tribune*, 6 July 1901, 8. A change was made to the lease agreement in Zion to bring it in line with the Law of Perpetuities. The leases would expire on 1 January 3000 (*Chicago Tribune*, 6 July 1901, 8.)

20. *Zion Banner*, 18 December 1901, 497.

21. *Port Pirie Recorder and North Western Mail*, 20 June 1906, 4. Figures supplied by Gladstone Dowie to Elder Harvey Brasefield.

22. Lindsay, *Life of John Alexander Dowie*, 144.

23 . Lindsay, *Life of John Alexander Dowie*,151.

24. Lindsay, *Life of John Alexander Dowie*,151.

25. *The Advertiser* (Adelaide), 3 July 1902, 9. For the Clibborns' relationship with Dowie, see Robinson, *The Holiness-Pentecostal Transition Years*.

26. *Leaves of Healing* 11: 607.

27. Dowie came under considerable criticism as Esther Dowie died without medical intervention. He responds to these criticisms in *Leaves of Healing* 11:133-134. A doctor was called but only to confirm the conclusions of Dr Speicher that nothing could be done for Esther. Dr Campbell testified to the coroner's court that it was "doubtful" if he could have saved Esther had he been called earlier.

28. Lindsay, *Life of John Alexander Dowie*, 154.

29. *Chicago Tribune*, 7 August 1902, 1.

30. *Chicago Tribune*, 8 August 1902, 3.

31. *True Republican*, 19 November 1902, 1.

32. *Leaves of Healing* 11: 606.

33. *Leaves of Healing* 11: 607.

34. *Leaves of Healing* 11: 768.

35. *Leaves of Healing* 11: 425.

36. Buckley, 'Dowie Analysed and Classified', 929.

37. *Christian Colonist*, 17 September 1886, 6.

38. Lindsay, *Life of John Alexander Dowie*, 157.

39. Buckley, 'Dowie Analysed and Classified', 930.

40. Buckley, 'Dowie Analysed and Classified', 930.

41. *Leaves of Healing* 12: 529; *Leaves of Healing* 14: 275-282.

42. *Wyoming Post Herald*, 11 November 1903, 6. On 12 June 1903, Dowie wrote to Alexander Boddy that he believed since in the former dispensation Priests had distinctive garments then "those who minister in divine things should have a distinctive garb or robe" (Boddy, 'A Visit to Zion City', 38).

43. *Leaves of Healing.* 11: 509.

44. Harlan, *John Alexander Dowie*, 13.

45. Harlan, *John Alexander Dowie*, 13.

46. Harlan, *John Alexander Dowie*, 15-16.

47. *Rock Island Argus*, 24 October 1903, 9.

48. Harlan, *John Alexander Dowie*, 18.

49. *Indianapolis News*, 12 October 1903, 19.

50. Cook, *Zion City*, 150.

51. Lindsay, *Life of John Alexander Dowie*, 160.

52. Harlan, *John Alexander Dowie*, 44.

53. Harlan adds as a footnote to his account of these events, "Mrs. Dowie told me that during his New York visitation he very greatly overworked being on the go from 5 am. until midnight taking charge of three large meetings each day and that his irritability was to be accounted for at least partially by this fact" (Harlan, *John Alexander Dowie*, 44).

54. *The Papyrus*, December 1903, 11.

55. *The Papyrus*, December 1903, 12.

56. *Leaves of Healing* 10: 276.

57. *New York Sun*, 20 October 1903, 2. The eight thousand figure was correct on seating in the venue but there was additional floor space for several thousand more.

58. *True Republican*, 24 October 1903, 3.

59. Jeanie was John Murray Dowie's niece. She did not comment publicly on her husband's allegations but later referred to a period of 6 months when she was removed from office in the church after telling Dowie he should apologise over an unspecified incident. The timeline would suggest her visit to Australia

coincided with this.

60. He remarried a widow in America, but this ended in divorce two years later. The divorce petition alleged he was "overbearing, repulsive and cruel" (*True Republican*, 28 January 1903, 6; *Indianapolis Journal*, 23 February 1903,1). John Murray received a $5,000 divorce payment. Dowie's ex-cook gives a "tell all" insider story of the domestic lives of the Dowie family and said the cause of the fight between the elder Dowie and his wife was because the two Mrs Dowies did not get on. According to Dowie's ex-employee, John Alexander Dowie was a tyrant; his wife could also be difficult; Gladstone had a temper as bad as his father, but "we loved Judge Dowie and Miss Esther" (*Indianapolis Journal*, 23 November 1903, 20).

61. *Leaves of Healing* 2: 466.

62. Quoted in *New York Evening World*, 26 October, 1903, 5.

63. It is not entirely clear that was the case, as John Murray Dowie appears to have repeated defended his son in any public statements and said the pressure of his work was the cause of Dowie's more outlandish behaviours.

64. *New York Sun*, 27 October, 1903, 3.

65. Newcomb, *Dowie, Anointed of the Lord*, 259-260. Andrew Dowie also claimed that his brother knew the history of his birth (*Register* (Adelaide) 1 August 1904, 4).

66. *Rock Island Argus*, 21 November 1903, 10.

67. *New York Sun*, 23 June 1906, 1.

68. Sheldrake, *Letters*, 246.

69. *New York Sun*, 1 November 1903, 8.

70. *Rock Island Argus*, 21 November 1903, 10.

71. *Leaves of Healing* 14: 145; *True Republican*, 4 November 1903, 3.

14. The wolf at the door

1. Dowie's followers had borrowed a reported $300, 000 dollars to 'loan' to him on top of other investments made (Harlan, *John Alexander Dowie*, 20).

2. *Chicago Tribune*, 25 November 1902, 7.

3. Cook, *Zion City*, 180.

4. *Leaves of Healing* 14: 197.

5. *Leaves of Healing* 14: 198.

6. *Republican-Atlas*, 11 December 1903, 14.

7. *True Republican*, 5 December 1903, 3.

8. *Rock Island Argus*, 3 December 1903, 1

9. *San Francisco Call*, 4 December 1903, 2.

10. *San Francisco Call*, 3 December 1903, 1.

11. *San Francisco Call*, 3 December 1903, 2.

12. *Rock Island Argus*, 7 December 1903, 1.

13. *Rock Island Argus*, 4 December 1903, 1.

14. *Leaves of Healing* 14: 221.

15. Arthur Newcomb in *San Francisco Call*, 20 January 1904, 16.

16. Lindsay, *Life of John Alexander Dowie*, 165.

17. *San Francisco Call*, 20 January 1904, 16; *Chicago Tribune* 9 April 1906, 2.

18. Cook, *Zion City*, 160-161.

19. Chant, 'The Australian Career of John Alexander Dowie', 21-27.

20. *True Republican*, 15 June 1904, 6.

21. *Times Dispatch*, July 01, 1904, 7.

22. Harlan referred to a letter he received from Henry Stevenson stating that Dowie suffered from dyspepsia and frequently couldn't keep food down but the "rank and file" did not know this (Harlan, *John Alexander Dowie*, 45).

23. Speicher, Barnes and Barnard claimed to have written to Dowie in April 1904 to warn him of his overspending and poor financial management (*Los Angeles Herald*, 16 April 1906, 9; Harlan, *John Alexander Dowie*, 21).

24. *Leaves of Healing* 15: 313.

25. *Leaves of Healing* 15: 357.

26. *Leaves of Healing* 15: 426.

27. *Leaves of Healing* 15: 426.

28. *Leaves of Healing* 15: 426.

29. *Leaves of Healing* 14: 825.

30. Lindsay, *Life of John Alexander Dowie*, 168.

31. *Leaves of Healing* 14: 798.

32. *Leaves of Healing* 14: 799.

33. *Leaves of Healing* 14: 799.

34. *Leaves of Healing* 16: 5.

35. *Salt Lake Telegram*, 4 March 1905. See also *Port Pirie Recorder* which reported on Voliva's statements of 5 April 1906 – "that God the Father, had ' the passion of a man and the 'immaculate conception of the Virgin Mary was the results of an actual physical act of the angel Gabriel who was also a man"

(*Port Pirie Recorder*, 20 June 1906, 4. Possibly by more than coincidence, Zion's Watchword for 1905 was "the Incarnation." (*Leaves of Healing* 16: 306).
36. Lindsay, *Life of John Alexander Dowie*, 168.
37. Lindsay, *Life of John Alexander Dowie*, 168.
38. Harlan, *John Alexander Dowie*, 19.
39. *Leaves of Healing* 18: 439 in Harlan, *John Alexander Dowie*, 20.
40. *Leaves of Healing* 15: 426, 591.
41. *Leaves of Healing* 16: 379.
42. *Leaves of Healing* 16: 165.
43. *Leaves of Healing* 3: 353-354, 366.
44. *Leaves of Healing* 16: 495-496.
45. *Leaves of Healing* 16: 526.
46. *Chicago Tribune*, 3 March 1905, 2.
47. *Chicago Tribune*, 3 March 1905, 2.
48. *Chicago Tribune*, 3 March 1905, 2.
49. *Leaves of Healing* 16: 658-666.
50. *Chicago Tribune*, 3 March 1905, 2.
51. *Chicago Tribune*, 3 March 1905, 2.
52. *Chicago Tribune*, 3 March 1905, 2.
53. *San Francisco Chronicle*, 6 March 1905, 7; *True Republican*, 12 April 1905, 6.
54. Cook, *Zion City*, 186.
55. Quoted in Lindsay, *Life of John Alexander Dowie*, 173.
56. Cook, *Zion City*, 157.
57. *True Republican*, 19 August , 1905,12; *Saturday Blade*, 26 August 1905, 8.
58. *Leaves of Healing* 7: 408.
59. Newcomb, *Dowie, Anointed of the Lord*, 246.
60. Newcomb, *Dowie, Anointed of the Lord*, 247.

15. The Accusers

1. Lindsay, *Life of John Alexander Dowie*, 171.
2. Lindsay, *Life of John Alexander Dowie*, 171.
3. *Evening Star* (Washington), 18 December 1905, 20; *True Republican*, 20 December 1905, 6.
4. Judge Barnes quoted in the *Saturday Blade*, 16 September 1905, 7.

5. *Evening Times Republican*, 20 December 1905, 5.
6. *Chicago Tribune* 18 January 1906, 3.
7 *Evening Times Republican*, 20 December 1905, 5.
8. *Chicago Tribune* 18 January 1906, 3.
9.*Chicago Tribune* 18 January 1906, 3.
10. *Rock Island Argus*, 22 January 1906, 1.
11. Cook, *Zion City*, 195.
12. Cook, *Zion City*, 197.
13. Figures quoted from Voliva in *Port Pirie Recorder and North Western Mail*, 20 June 1906, 4.
14. *Chicago Tribune* 9 April 1906, 2.
15. *St John Daily Sun*, 3 April 1906,1.
16. *St John Daily Sun*, 3 April 1906,1.
17. *St John Daily Sun*, 3 April 1906, 1.
18. *St John Daily Sun*, 3 April 1906, 1.
19. *Rock Island Argus*, 3 April 1906, 1; *New York Tribune*, 10 April 1906, 2.
20. *St John Daily Sun*, 3 April 1906, 1.
21. *Los Angeles Herald*, 4 April 1906, 1.
22. *Los Angeles Herald*, 21 June 1906, 2.
23. *Chicago Tribune*, 7 April 1906, 2. Dowie denied all allegations of polygamy, *San Francisco Call*, 6 April 1906, 2.
24. *Sacramento Union*, 4 April 1906, 1.
25. *Chicago Tribune* 9 April 1906, 2.
26. Ruth Hofer travelled to America with Dowie and his family after the World Tour. The other woman mentioned was a Miss Harriet Ware who was expelled from Zion with her mother. Dowie claimed his only dealings with Miss Ware were when he felt she was being led astray by her music teacher. Miss Hofer was innocent of any wrong doing and any letters between them were of a purely paternal nature (*Evening Star* (Washington), 9 April 1906, 13).
27. *Evening Star* (Washington), 6 April 1906, 17.
28. *New York Times*, 12 April 1906. Dowie's messages had been taken as promoting polygamy as early as 1903 - see *Truth* (Sydney) 11 October 1903, 5.
29. *Chicago Tribune*, 7 April 1906, 2.
30. *Chicago Tribune*, 7 April 1906, 2.

31. *New York Tribune*, 10 April 1906, 2.

32. *Chicago Tribune*, 7 April 1906, 2. Mrs Ware planned to write about her experiences in Zion and referred to the mysterious "seven vestal virgins project." These women were supposed to follow Dowie around carrying torches of fire.

33. *Chicago Tribune*, 7 April 1906, 2.

34. *Rock Island Argus*, 22 June 1906, 1.

35. Cook, *Zion City*, 257, no 37.

36. *Chicago Tribune*, 7 April 1906, 2.

37. *Evening Times-Republican*, 27 June, 1904, 5.

38. *Evening Star* (Washington), 9 April 1906, 13.

39. *Urbana Daily Courier*, 5 April 1906, 1.

40. *St John Daily Sun*, 9 April 1906, 1.

41. *St John Daily Sun*, 9 April 1906, 1.

42. *St John Daily Sun*, 9 April 1906, 1.

43. *San Francisco Call*, April 10, 1906, 3.

44. *San Francisco Call*, April 10, 1906, 3.

45. *St John Daily Sun*, 9 April 1906, 1.

46. *The Age* (Melbourne) 28 May 1906, 5.

47. *Chicago Tribune* 9 April 1906, 2.

48. *True Republican*, 18 April 1906, 3.

49. *Evening Star* (Washington), 9 April 1906, 13.

50. *Evening Star* (Washington), 9 April 1906, 13.

51. *Evening Star* (Washington), 9 April 1906, 13.

52. *Chicago Tribune*, 7 April 1906, 3.

53. *Fulton County News*, 11 April 1906, 2.

54. *Evening Times Republican*, 6 April 1906, 1.

55. *San Francisco Call*, 10 April 1906, 3.

56. *Ottumwa Courier*, 14 April 1906, 6.

57. *Ottumwa Courier*, 14 April 1906, 6; *New York Sun* 8 April 1906, 2.

58. *Los Angeles Herald*, 11 April 1906, 2.

59. *Los Angeles Herald*, 11 April 1906, 2.

60. *Los Angeles Herald*, 11 April 1906, 2.

61. *San Francisco Chronicle*, 3 April 1906, 2.

62. Lindsay, *Life of John Alexander Dowie*, 175.

63. *Los Angeles Times*, 29 April, 1.
64. *True Republican*, 16 May 1906, 6.
65. Cook, *Zion City*, 206.
66. *Sacramento Union*, 29 April 1906, 1.
67. *Los Angeles Herald*, 14 April 1906, 1.
68. *Rock Island Argus*, 28 June 1906, 1.
69. *Rock Island Argus*, 28 June 1906, 1.
70. *New York Times*, 21 June 1906, 5.
71. *Waterloo Daily Courier*, 15 June 1906 7.
72. *Waterloo Daily Courier*, 15 June 1906 7.
73. *Rock Island Argus*, 27 June 1906, 1.
74. *Rock Island Argus* 21 June 1906, 1.
75. Pietrusza, *Judge Kenesaw Mountain Landis*, 46.

16. Last days

1. *Rock Island Argus*, 14 November 1906, 7.
2. See Voliva's statements in the Zion Banner where he refers to his former allies as "cornered rats" fighting for their share of Zion's money (*Zion Banner*, 2 August 1907, 4.)
3. For a useful summary of Voliva and the early Pentecostals in Zion see 'The Historic Legacy of Zion's Christian Assembly in the Beginning', available online at http://www.christianassemblyzion.org/SiteFiles/105903/Content/Images/History.pdf. On his visit to Zion, Alexander Boddy went to hear a Voliva sermon and called it "A Christless address" full of references to the Devil and with no mention of Christ. He thought Voliva might have been studying Jesse Penn-Lewis' *War on the Saints* ('A Visit to Zion City', *Confidence*, 37).
4. *True Republican*, 24 October 1906, 6. The tragic death of Letitia Greenhaulgh doubtless assisted Voliva's attempts to eject Parham's followers (*Los Angeles Herald*, 21 September 1907, 1; *Chicago Tribune*, 23 September 1907, 5).
5. *Chicago Tribune*, 5 September 1906, 5.
6. *True Republican*, 26 September 1906, 2.
7. *Rock Island Argus*, 10 October 1906.1.
8. *Urbana Daily Courier*, 24 September 1906, 2.

9. *New York Tribune*, 17 November 1906, 12.
10. Lindsay, *Life of John Alexander Dowie*, 179-180.
11. *True Republican*, 8 May 1912, 1.
12. Lindsay, *Life of John Alexander Dowie*, 180.
13. *True Republican*, 13 March 1907, 3.
14. *Rockford Daily Register*, 28 December 1906, 4.
15. Gardiner, 'Story of John Alexander Dowie', 14. The *Chicago Tribune* reported a Mr J.W. Lawrence healed of a crippling illness of 3 years standing (*Chicago Tribune* 27 August 1906, 14).

Epilogue

1. *Leaves of Healing* 14: 681.
2. *Sunday Star* (Washington), 17 March 1907, 4.
3. Lindsay believed Dowie prophesied radio in 1897 and television in 1904 (Lindsay, *Life of John Alexander Dowie*, 133-134). However radio wave technology was on show at the 1893 Chicago World Fair and television at the 1900 Paris World Fair, predating Dowie's statements on both.
4. *Leaves of Healing* 12: 244.
5. Brumback, *Suddenly ... from Heaven*, 10.
6. Taylor, 'Publish and Be Blessed', 73.
7. Tomlinson, *Diary of A. J. Tomlinson*, 19.
8. 'Margaret Cantel' in *The New International Dictionary of Pentecostal and Charismatic Movements*, 454.
9. Chapman, 'The Role of Woman in Early Pentecostalism', 134.
10. *Leaves of Healing* 6: 8.
11. Van der Laan, 'Discerning the Body: An Analysis of Pentecostalism in the Netherlands', 34.
12. Hubbard, *Dowie*, 108-9.
13. *Bulletin of the Illinois State Board of Health*, Vol 2 (1906), 187-188.
14. Lindsay, *Life of John Alexander Dowie*, 184.
15. Boddy, 'A Visit to Zion City', *Confidence*, 36.
16. Wilks, *Edward Irving*, 285.
17. Lindsay, *Life of John Alexander Dowie*, 132.
18. Stanley, 'Edinburgh and World Christianity', 88.

He sendeth His word and healeth them.

Printed in Great
Britain
by Amazon